BARBECUE THE BEARD WAY

is fun for everyone—those who do the cooking and those who do the eating. Proving that you can have variety and keep the cooking easy, he adds sauces from faraway places to the standard barbecue fare. Try one from the Creole country or another based on Chinese cooking. In addition to hamburgers and steak, grill veal, turkey and venison, shrimp and lobsters for a delicious change. James Beard also tailors the desserts to the outdoor scene—for example, an adaptation of strawberry shortcake that is simple and superb.

And to round off your menu, there are recipes for a host of complements from the kitchen—dishes prepared indoors and then brought out to make the meal something to remember.

It's relaxed,
casual and very good eating when you

BARBECUE WITH BEARD.

Books by James Beard

Barbecue With Beard
James Beard's Fish Cookery
The Best of Beard

Published by
WARNER BOOKS

ATTENTION: SCHOOLS AND CORPORATIONS

WARNER books are available at quantity discounts with bulk
purchase for educational, business, or sales promotional use. For
information, please write to: SPECIAL SALES DEPARTMENT,
WARNER BOOKS, 75 ROCKEFELLER PLAZA, NEW YORK, N.Y.
10019

ARE THERE WARNER BOOKS
YOU WANT BUT CANNOT FIND IN YOUR LOCAL STORES?

You can get any WARNER BOOKS title in print. Simply send title
and retail price, plus 50¢ per order and 20¢ per copy to cover
mailing and handling costs for each book desired. New York State
and California residents add applicable sales tax. Enclose check
or money order only, no cash please, to: WARNER BOOKS, P.O.
BOX 690, NEW YORK, N.Y. 10019

BARBECUE WITH BEARD

Outdoor Recipes From A Great Cook

BY JAMES BEARD

WARNER BOOKS

A Warner Communications Company

WARNER BOOKS EDITION

Copyright © 1975 by Western Publishing Company, Inc.
All rights reserved

Recipes in this edition previously appeared in **Jim Beard's Barbecue Cookbook** © 1958, 1959, 1964, 1965 by Maco Magazine Corporation and **Jim Beard's Complete Book of Barbecue and Rotisserie Cooking** © 1954 by Maco Magazine Corporation.

This Warner Books Edition is published by arrangement with Western Publishing Company, Inc.

Cover design by Gene Light

Cover photograph by Jerry West

Warner Books, Inc., 75 Rockefeller Plaza, New York, N.Y. 10019

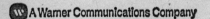 A Warner Communications Company

Printed in the United States of America

First Printing: June, 1976

Reissued: July, 1981

10 9 8 7 6 5 4 3

CONTENTS

FROM THE OUTDOORS

KNOW-HOW
& EQUIPMENT

KNOW-HOW

What originated as a vogue for outdoor cookery is today an integral part of American family life. It is no longer a novelty to grill over charcoal or to roast on an electrically driven spit; it is part and parcel of our living pattern. In those parts of the country where indoor-outdoor living is not possible the year around, many designers and architects are creating charcoal units to go into their new houses.

This is an age of simplified living. It is also an age of simplified eating. Grilled and spitted roasted foods are delicious, nutritious, and high in protein—attributes that are making them increasingly popular with a growing number of American families.

Fire Building

Charcoal cooking has achieved tremendous success, but many of its most ardent admirers wear themselves out before the meal trying to make a proper fire. This is basically a simple task, but a bit of study and practice is needed.

Charcoal briquets are the most satisfactory and efficient type of fuel that I have found. You can buy other briquets of various substances, but they are not as satisfactory—in fact, some of them give off so much heat that they may damage expensive equipment. Wood charcoal is a good fuel but not as economical as charcoal briquets.

Briquets should be dry, so always keep them in a dry place. Damp or wet briquets not only create smoke but they take much longer to ignite and to build up to usable coals.

For kindling, the most satisfactory method is an odorless paint thinner or some other specially labeled fire starter. Build up 35 to 40 briquets, pyramid fashion, apply your paint thinner, and wait 5 minutes before igniting. Briquets take about 30 minutes to get burning satisfactorily. One indication that they are burning properly will be the formation of a little white ash on your coals.

By all means, avoid making the fire too big—let the size of the food to be cooked determine the dimensions of the fire. Be sure to spread it evenly so that it extends just beyond the meat.

The number of briquets should depend on the size of your unit. A portable grill may take from 15 to 25 briquets, but a larger wheeled unit may require up to 45. Additional fuel may be added later, if needed.

The way to control the heat is to keep your fire level. Broiling temperature is always higher than that for roasting and should be around 350°F. at grill level. Varying temperatures are to be avoided. Sear the meat close to the coals but then keep it at a distance.

Seasoning

Outdoor cooks disagree as to when is the best time to salt the meat. My advice is not to salt it until it is almost done, as the salt may start the juices running too early in the cooking process.

Avoid unnecessary basting, particularly with highly seasoned sauces. The flavor of the meat will come through naturally if you baste it in its own juices while it is cooking.

Balancing the Meat

Achieving the proper balance when roasting is the mark of the expert outdoor chef. If you watch an efficient operation you can't help but notice the care with which the veteran ties and trusses, always making certain that the meat is securely fixed. He will then pass the spit through the heaviest part, so that it is perfectly balanced, before he even applies his holding forks. If he fails to balance the meat properly, he will remove it from the spit and try again.

This is the only way to ensure the right balance, and knowing how to achieve it will double your proficiency at the grill.

EQUIPMENT

Many people put a lot of time and money into assembling equipment for outdoor cookery and constructing elaborate outdoor kitchens in their yards or patios. Though this can be fun for the ambitious handyman, it's not necessary. There are many portable grills and braziers on the market that will give you just as tasty a result as the most complicated "made-to-order" job.

If you do have the money, space, and desire to build an elaborate outdoor grill with ovens, spits, storage units, and accessories, here are a few points to remember:

If you live in a cold climate, lay your foundation below the frost line to prevent cracking and crumbling.

Have electrical outlets placed near your outdoor grill if possible. This enables you to make use of electrical rotisseries, fryers, coffee makers, mixers, and many other items that will speed and simplify your cooking.

Make provision for cooking on a spit. This is the most delicious way to cook large cuts of meat and poultry. There are portable spits on the market that can be attached to an outdoor grill in the summer and used indoors in the fireplace in the winter. Some rotisseries are complete portable spitting units in themselves and can be used on the patio, in the kitchen, in the playroom—any place where you have an electrical outlet.

As I've said, it's not necessary to build a complicated outdoor kitchen in order to have delectable feasts. A friend of mine does very well with a unit he built from an old oil can and some discarded grills from a bank teller's window. Many of us have had some of our most memorable meals cooked over an open campfire with a simple grill on top. The portable equipment you can buy today includes everything from the simplest charcoal container up to elaborate pushmobiles that are both glamorous and efficient.

Grills

Portable Grills

There are two different types of portable grill:

1. The Japanese *hibachi*, while a little ponderous to transport in a car, is ideal for small terraces or inside the house itself for grilling steaks, chops, and hors d'oeuvres. On the same idea, there are also lighter and folding portable grills.

2. Then there is a small, heavy-duty type of portable grill that comes in a carrying case and can be transported along with its fuel.

Wheeled Grills

The market for this kind of grill is an ever growing one. Probably the most popular of all of these is a wheeled brazier type of grill which comes in various sizes and at various prices. Some of these brazier types have hoods attached and many have spits. A few are equipped with electrically driven spits. The brazier type that has an adjustable firebox is a most satisfactory unit for most families, as it does a really efficient grilling job.

The vertical type of grill is usually equipped with two fireboxes and a drip pan underneath. This means that the meat to be grilled is hung between them and cooks on both sides at once. There is also a multiple-spitted grill for people who enjoy cooking on skewers. Many other types are specially designed to be installed in kitchens or recreation rooms. These are complete with hoods and exhaust fans. Charcoal cookery is not the chore it used to be.

Electric Equipment

Electric Rotisserie

If you do not have an electrically driven spit with your outdoor unit, you may use your household rotisseries —in fact, some brands are much more practical for outdoor use and can handle a 30-pound turkey, or have 7 or 8 skewers which will take a variety of meats and fish or a 5- or 6-rib roast of beef.

Electric Skillets and Saucepans

Electric skillets have become an invaluable assistant to the outdoor grill. The electric skillet is useful for vegetables, sauces, desserts, casserole dishes, and such pleasant outdoor morsels as *sukiyaki*. The electric saucepan, which doubles as a French fryer, enables you to cook many pleasant accompaniments to your grill on the scene.

Aids to Barbecuing

Certain necessities and a few luxuries are very pleasant to have. I don't believe in being the gadget type of outdoor cook, but I am exceedingly fond of good equipment. Among the necessities we will list:

● Electric outlets near your cooking space. These are necessary for using electrically driven units and electric equipment which may be called auxiliary to the main units.

● Asbestos gloves and leather or canvas work gloves should both be kept at the cooking site. Gloves are much better than tongs for handling charcoal. Asbestos gloves are invaluable for handling hot spits and pieces of equipment.

● Foil has many uses in outdoor cooking. For instance, if you line the bottom of a portable grill or the fireplace of a large grill with several layers of heavy-duty aluminum foil, it will: Reflect back heat on the food and speed cooking; cut down your consumption of briquets and help to make a more even temperature; leave a clean firebox when you envelop the ashes, and catch any grease which has dripped through.

Furthermore, foil may be used to wrap meats, vegetables, game birds, fish, poultry, and fruits—in short, anything that is to be cooked over charcoal or in the ashes. It is invaluable to the camper and the outdoor griller. It is also a perfect receptacle in which to carry any type of food to a picnic or camping site. It may be used as a container for freezing or for roasting or broiling.

● I strongly urge the use of tongs rather than a fork when working at the grill. Tongs allow you to handle meat and vegetables without piercing them as the fork does. I cannot overemphasize the importance of having several heavy-duty units of this type.

● Thermometers. Charcoal cookery has become so scientific that temperature is of major importance. A spit thermometer, with which some grills are now equipped, is invaluable. A grill thermometer is another piece of equipment that you will find useful at all times. The third adjunct is a meat thermometer, and for this I recommend one which has a dial that is marked from zero to 220°F. I do not happen to agree with some of the temperatures recommended for meat by various authorities in this field, and I wouldn't be surprised if, after you start comparing, you disagreed, too.

● I find that a bottle equipped with a sprinkler top, like the ones used to sprinkle clothes, is a necessity next to the grill when a bit of fat or oil drops into the firebox, causing a sudden conflagration.

● Basters. I have seen Puerto Ricans and Mexicans use cornhusks for basting, and—much to my disgust—I've even seen string dish mops used. There are plenty of good basting brushes on the market, so just look around for one that performs the job efficiently.

● Broiling baskets—holders. Hinged broilers and broiling baskets, including one with a small mesh for broiling small fish and meats, are useful to the active outdoor cook. Three or four of these should be in your prop box.

● Many broilers and grills now come equipped with drip pans. These are helpful in preventing small conflagrations and they also catch some of the delicious juices that drip from roasts and grills.

● Skewers. There is a tremendous variety of skewers on the market, but many of them are too long to be practical and others are much too frail. The ones with wooden handles are excellent. There is also an all-metal type that is quite short but exceedingly efficient. The very short ones are good for hors d'oeuvres as well as for roasts. For certain purposes bamboo chopsticks make handy tools, and long metal knitting needles are useful adjuncts when spitting small birds for the grill.

● A heavy-duty cutting board and good knives are necessities for the outdoor griller. You will probably use your regular kitchen knives, but be sure they are

15

good and sharp. There is no need for the fancy gadget set of outdoor knife sets.

- A large pepper mill and a salt grinder or a very large shaker are absolute necessities.
- Towels and pot holders are welcomed by most good cooks.
- Other equipment includes skillets, big trays, cook-all baskets, serving spoons, and various items which may be borrowed from your kitchen.

GRILLING &
BROILING

The simplest way of cooking meat, fish and fowl—and one of the most delicious—is by direct heat. It can be done with any kind of grill, fixed or folding, that holds the meat at the right cooking distance from a bed of glowing charcoal or hardwood coals. You can also do your broiling under the broiler of an electric range or portable grill, or under the broiler in a gas range —in case you need to bring your barbecue party indoors because of rain, or want to have your party in the kitchen out of the summer season.

Another style of broiling which will produce good results with many of the recipes in this chapter— though without imparting the extra flavor you get from glowing coals or infra-red rays—is pan-broiling. It's not usually the first-choice method for my tastes, but it will work well with beef when other methods of broiling aren't practicable. Methods for pan-broiling meats are specified in this chapter.

BEEF
Steak

Beefsteak is probably the most popular meat in America, and certainly nothing is heartier or more satisfying than a good big steak, thick and juicy, and sizzling hot right from the grill.

To Broil a Steak

Prepare the fire as recommended on page 7. When it has become good white coals, and when your grill level registers about 350°F. to 370°F., sear the steak on both sides to retain the juices throughout the grilling. Then lower the fire bed and continue cooking, turning over with the tongs until the proper degree of doneness is reached (see chart on pages 20–21). To char the steak, bring the coals up to the meat and flame it before serving. Add salt and pepper just before the steak is done.

To Pan-Broil a Steak

Some people prefer to cook steak in a skillet, and some steaks are better prepared in a skillet. For this method, use a heavy cast-iron or cast-aluminum pan and get it sizzling hot. Cut off a little of the beef fat and grease the skillet lightly—or just sprinkle the pan with salt. Pop in the steak and sear it quickly on both sides. Turn the meat frequently and keep pouring off any excess fat. Season to taste just before serving and add a good dab of butter.

Amounts to Buy

Figure ¾ to 1 pound of steak per person. Have the steaks cut 1 to 3 inches thick, with excess fat removed. Frozen steaks may be cooked without thawing. Try not to choose a steak too large for your cooking facilities.

You may find individual steaks the most satisfactory, particularly if you have a space problem.

The Best Cuts

Good beef is a cherry-red color when fresh and a purplish hue when well aged. The flesh of steaks should be well marbled with fat and edged with firm, flaky, cream-colored fat. The top grade is stamped U.S. Prime on the untrimmed cuts; the next best grade is stamped U.S. Choice.

You will find very good aged beef in some supermarkets. Order your extra-special steaks well in advance and get a properly aged one, which is tenderer than strictly fresh meat and has a slightly gamy flavor. The best steaks for grilling and broiling are these:

Porterhouse This cut comes from the short loin section of the loin and has a cross-shaped bone in the middle. The fillet is on one side of the bone and the contra-fillet on the other. It is probably the choicest cut of steak. For outdoor cooking, order it cut extra-thick—1½ to 3 inches.

T-Bone This is practically the same cut as porterhouse, except that it is further up the loin. It has less tenderloin than porterhouse.

Sirloin This is a fine cut from lower down the loin than porterhouse. It is excellent eating and economical for a large group. Have it cut not less than 1¼ inches thick. In England and France this cut is preferred for roasting, being considered far better than the rib cut generally used in this country.

Rib Steaks These are called *entrecôte* by the French, and considered a delicacy. They are best when cut from the first three ribs. Have them cut with or without the bone, as you choose.

Minute Steaks These are very thin steaks, cut from the rib, the sirloin, or the shell. You will have better results if you pan-broil or sauté them quickly than if you grill them directly over the coals.

Also available are minute steaks which are cut thinner than usual. They are from ⅓ to 1 inch thick and may be cut from any of the parts of the loin we have

19

mentioned. They generally provide 5 to 10 ounces of meat. Broil them quickly over a hot grill or sauté them in butter in a hot skillet on the grill. They must be very rare to be worth eating.

Shell Steaks These are cut from the contra-fillet—the half of the porterhouse that is left when the fillet has been removed. They are the best choice if you want to serve individual steaks.

Fillet This is really the tenderest part of the tenderloin. If you are serving several people, it is best to buy the whole tenderloin and either cut it yourself into individual steaks or cook it whole. Or you can cut part of it into steaks and spit and roast the rest. You will find it cheaper per pound when you buy it in a whole piece.

Flank Steak This is a triangular piece of meat which many people feel is not suitable for grilling. If properly grilled and carved, however, it is one of the most luscious bits of beef that can be had.

Other Cuts

Some of the less expensive grades of steak, such as chuck blade, top round, and rump, as well as short ribs, may be broiled if they are first marinated.

To cook chunks of beef on skewers, the best choice is sirloin, though the cheaper cuts may be used if marinated to make them tender. Buy beef for this purpose by the piece and cut it into cubes yourself.

Steak Timetable

1 INCH	Very rare—8 minutes Rare—9 minutes Medium—12 minutes Well done—15-18 minutes
1½ INCHES	Very rare—8-10 minutes Rare—10-12 minutes Medium—13-15 minutes Well done—15-20 minutes

2 INCHES	Very rare—14-18 minutes Rare—18-25 minutes Medium—25-32 minutes Well done—30-45 minutes
2½ INCHES	Very rare—20-25 minutes Rare—25-35 minutes Medium—35-40 minutes Well-done—45-60 minutes or more
3 INCHES OR MORE	Should be cooked with a meat thermometer inserted in the thickest part. Use the following temperature table: Very rare—120°-130°F. Rare—125°-135°F. Medium—145°-155°F. Well done—160°-170°F.

The only way to make absolutely certain that a steak is cooked the way you want it is to use the age-old knife test. With a sharp knife cut a small incision in the flesh next to the bone and see how red it is. Warning: If night has fallen, use a good flashlight to check the color.

Steak Specialties

Barbecued Steak

Make a paste of 2 to 3 teaspoons of dry mustard, salt to taste, and enough bourbon or other whisky to moisten. Broil as usual.

Steak Rosemary

Cover both sides of the steak with rosemary pressed in with the heel of your hand. Grill as usual and season just before serving. Add a good pat of butter.

Pepper Steak

Use cracked pepper, or crush your own from whole peppercorns with a rolling pin or mortar and pestle. Press the pepper into the steak on both sides. Let it stand for an hour. Grill as usual, salting as you turn the steak. When done, flame with ¼ cup of cognac.

Churrasco

This South American version of beefsteak is wonderfully good eating.

Buy a large sirloin of 7 pounds or more, about 3 inches thick. Or you can use two steaks with a combined weight of 7 or more pounds. Broil the steak according to previous instructions and during the cooking baste once or twice with butter seasoned to taste with dried rosemary. Cook the meat just to the rare state and char it at the last minute.

To serve: Cut the steak in rather thin diagonal slices and put them in the Churrasco Sauce (below) for a minute. Serve each person some of the sauce with the meat. Good accompaniments for this dish are home fried potatoes, sautéed or roasted onions, and French bread with butter.

Serves 6.

Churrasco Sauce

2 cups finely chopped green onions	1 tablespoon freshly ground pepper
½ pound butter	1 cup white wine
Dash of rosemary (approximately)	½ cup wine vinegar
1½ teaspoons salt	Large lump of butter

Sauté the green onions in the butter until just soft. Add a dash or two of rosemary, the salt, pepper, wine, and vinegar. Bring this to a boil, lower the heat, and simmer for 5 minutes. Taste for seasoning and add the lump of butter.

Makes about 4 cups sauce.

Variation
Substitute any other steak or a slice of rare rib roast of beef and serve it in the same manner.

Beefsteak Jérome le Plat

In spite of the French name, this dish was originally Italian. The secret is in the sauce. As a base, use your favorite recipe for hollandaise sauce.
Broil the steak of your choice in your favorite manner, slice it diagonally, and bathe the slices in the sauce below.

Sauce Jérome le Plat

1   cup hollandaise sauce
    Juice of 1 lemon
2   tablespoons tomato
    puree
1   teaspoon freshly ground
    pepper

Dash of Worcestershire
sauce
¼ cup finely chopped
    parsley

When the hollandaise has thickened, stir in the lemon juice, tomato puree, pepper, and Worcestershire. Just before serving, add the parsley.

Makes about 1¼ cups sauce.

Beefsteak Pizzaioula

This is another Italian version of steak, popular with those who like the flavor of tomatoes.

1 sirloin or rib steak (2 inches thick, 3 to 4 pounds) Pizzaioula Sauce (below)	Finely chopped Italian parsley Sautéed mushrooms

Broil the steak according to instructions (page 12) to the desired degree of doneness. Remove to a hot platter.

To serve: Pour the sauce over the steak and top it with the parsley and mushrooms.

Serves 4 to 6.

Pizzaioula Sauce

4 cloves garlic, chopped	Salt and freshly ground pepper
¼ cup olive oil	to taste
1 can (33 ounces) Italian tomatoes	1 teaspoon oregano

Sauté the garlic in the olive oil until soft. Add the tomatoes and cook down to half the original amount. Season to taste with the salt, pepper, and oregano.

Makes about 1¾ cups sauce.

Roquefort Broiled Steak

The cheese spread should melt into a most pleasing sauce for the steak when it is done.

1 large clove garlic
½ pound Roquefort cheese
4 tablespoons butter, softened
2 teaspoons dry mustard

Dash of Worcestershire sauce
1 steak (your choice)

Crush the garlic with a heavy fork in a small bowl. Add the Roquefort and butter. Cream together well and flavor with the mustard and Worcestershire.

Grill your steak as usual. When you are turning it, spread the browned side with the cheese mixture. It will melt as the second side of the steak cooks.

Makes about 1¼ cups spread.

Filet Mignon with Tarragon Butter

Figure on two small filet mignons per person. They should be about 1 inch thick. Brush them well with oil and broil to a rare stage over charcoal.

To serve: Remove the filets to a hot platter or board and top each with Tarragon Butter (below).

Tarragon Butter

¼ pound butter
1 teaspoon dry mustard
1½ teaspoons tarragon

Dash of freshly ground pepper

Cream the ingredients together until fluffy and well mixed.

Makes 8 tablespoons flavored butter.

Sliced Larded Tenderloin on French Bread

For hearty appetites allow 1 pound of tenderloin for each guest. Be sure to get whole, not sliced, fillet. Ask the butcher to lard the fillets for you (if you have a larding needle you can do it yourself). For each fillet, soak three thin strips of salt pork in cognac for 2 hours. Run them through the edges of the beef with the larding needle.

Roll the whole fillets in coarsely crushed black pepper and broil over coals for about 25 minutes, turning often. Season to taste with salt. Or you can spit them and roast over charcoal for the same length of time. If you use a meat thermometer, remove the fillets at 120°F. They will be very rare—the way they taste best.

To serve: Cream ½ pound of butter and blend it with 1½ to 2 teaspoons of rosemary. Heat French bread and split the loaf. Spread each half liberally with the rosemary butter. Cut the fillet into paper-thin slices and arrange them on the hot buttered French bread. Guests can eat them as sandwiches or with knife and fork.

Steak Sandwiches

You may use any preferred large steak, cut thick, for steak sandwiches. Grill it as you normally would, and when it is done, cut it in thin slices and serve between pieces of warmed or toasted French bread well buttered.

An excellent way to make steak sandwiches for a crowd is to buy a whole tenderloin. Tell your butcher you're going to cook it whole and have him trim it for you. Oil it or grease it well with butter, place it on a grill over hot coals. Turn it often and baste constantly with additional fat, for the tenderloin will take from 10 to 25 minutes to cook to a delicious rare state. Season it before or during cooking and serve in thin slices, on French bread as above.

Châteaubriand Marchand de Vin

Since a Châteaubriand has no fat, it is at its best only when served with a sauce.

A Châteaubriand is the most luxurious cut from the center part of the fillet. It should be very thick and weigh from 1 to 2 pounds. Buy marrow bones and have the butcher cut them so that the marrow can be extracted in one piece.

Broil the Châteaubriands. During the cooking, brush them frequently with melted butter and turn them often. Meanwhile, extract the marrow and slice it in thin rounds. Poach for about 1 minute in boiling salted water.

To serve: When the meat is done to your satisfaction, remove it to hot plates, pour the Sauce for Châteaubriand (below) over each portion; top with slices of poached marrow.

Sauce for Châteaubriand

⅔ cup finely chopped
  green onions
¼ pound butter
1 cup red wine
  (preferably a good
  Bordeaux)

1 can (15 ounces)
  brown gravy
  Dash of cognac
  Large pat of butter
  Juice of 1 lemon
  Chopped parsley

Sauté the green onions in the ¼ pound butter until just colored. Add the wine and cook this down to half its volume. Add the brown gravy and simmer to heat through. Add the cognac, pat of butter, and lemon juice. Just before serving, sprinkle the sauce heavily with the parsley.

Makes about 2¾ cups sauce.

Marinated Steak

You can broil the less tender cuts, such as chuck blade and top round, with delicious results by first marinating the meat.

1	cup olive oil	1	teaspoon freshly
	Juice of 1 lemon		ground pepper
1	clove garlic, crushed	1	top round or
	Dash of salt		chuck blade steak

Mix all ingredients and pour over the steak, turning it several times to make sure it is evenly coated. Let stand in a warm place for several hours or overnight. Grill as usual, omitting seasoning.

Makes about 1¼ cups marinade.

London Broil

1 flank steak (about 2 pounds)
Salt and freshly ground pepper to taste

Have the butcher trim the steak well. Broil it quickly, allowing 3 to 4 minutes to a side, until it is nicely charred on the outside and still juicy red in the middle. Season to taste with salt and pepper and remove it to a hot platter.

To serve: Cut the steak on the diagonal, holding the knife so that it slopes from left to right at about a 30° angle with the cutting surface.

Serves 4.

Oriental Flank Steak

½ cup sherry
½ cup soy sauce
2 cloves garlic,
chopped

¼ cup chopped gingerroot
or 1 teaspoon ground
ginger
1 flank steak
(about 2 pounds)

Combine the sherry, soy sauce, garlic, and gingerroot. Soak the steak in this marinade for several hours, turning frequently. Grill and carve as for London Broil (above).

Serves 4.

Chili-Oriental Flank Steak
Add 1 tablespoon of chili powder to the marinade for Oriental Flank Steak (above). Marinate, grill, and carve in the same manner.

Serves 4.

Minute Steaks

Allow ½ pound of minute steaks for each guest. The steaks should not be over ½ inch thick, and they must be pan-broiled or sautéed. Be sure the pan is sizzling hot, grease it lightly with butter or fat, pop in the steaks, and cook quickly—about 1 minute to a side. Season to taste and remove to hot plates.

To serve: Place over hot buns and cover with French sauce, rings of raw onions marinated in oil and vinegar, or sautéed mushrooms.

Sauced Minute Steaks

Cook minute steaks as above. Remove them to a hot platter and keep them warm. To the pan add 2 tablespoons of butter, a good dash of Worcestershire sauce, and ⅓ cup of red wine. Bring to a brisk boil and pour over the steaks.

Shortribs

I find that broiled Prime or Choice grade shortribs are a very pleasant change from other meats. They are sturdy and not always as tender as other meats, but they have a delicious flavor. If I am buying a large roast beef, I usually have it cut short and use the ends of the ribs for broiling. Or sometimes it is possible to get an excellent piece of shortrib from the butcher.

Broiled Shortribs in Red Wine Marinade

5 pounds shortribs Prepared mustard	½ cup chopped parsley Red wine
2 cloves garlic, finely chopped	2 or 3 bay leaves
1 teaspoon dried basil or ¼ cup finely chopped fresh basil	

Brush the shortribs with the mustard. Put the ribs in a shallow pan and sprinkle with the garlic and basil. Add the parsley and cover with red wine. Add the bay leaves and marinate for 24 hours.

Remove the shortribs from the marinade, dry on paper towels, and broil slowly until the ribs are well browned and crisp on the outside.

To serve: Accompany with fresh horseradish grated into sour cream and tiny new potatoes steamed in butter.

Serves 4.

Deviled Beef Bones

If you have any leftover meat from a beef rib dish, you have the makings of a delectable dish. Cut the rib bones apart, dip them in beaten egg and then in dry bread crumbs, and cook very quickly in a large skillet with plenty of butter. As soon as the pieces are brown and crisp and hot through, serve them with a pungent sauce or deviled sauce (see pages 196–210). They should be eaten with the fingers, of course—with plenty of large paper napkins on hand.

Burgers and Franks

Once upon a time, before the Pizza Age, hamburgers and frankfurters were the most popular foods in the country. There are few things better than hamburger, if it is seasoned properly, cooked just right, and served up hot and rare.

You'll also find some suggestions for burgers made from ingredients other than beef. I recommend you try them for a pleasant change of routine.

I am old fashioned. I still like frankfurters with skin, and hunt them down ferociously. Hot dogs are also indispensable to the outdoor grill—in fact, you couldn't maintain one without them.

If you're throwing a party with a menu based on burgers and franks, you might like to include some of the Grilled Sandwiches on pages 154–158 as a zippy accompaniment.

Plain Hamburgers

Buy lean ground beef with no more than 25 to 30 per cent fat and allow at least ½ pound per person. If you are serving hamburgers on buns, make two patties of ¼ pound each per person. The less you handle the raw meat, the juicier the cooked hamburger will be, so form the patties gently with a light touch. Shape the hamburgers around a cube of ice. The grilling melts the ice and leaves the meat juicy. Brush the patties with melted butter butter or oil. Sear them well on both sides and then continue grilling, turning often, until they are done as you like them. Personally, I feel they should be crusty brown on the outside but still juicy and rare in the middle. Season with salt and pepper as you turn.

To serve: Place the hamburgers on hot toasted buns or hot toasted French bread with a choice of good radishes and pickles. Don't forget the mustard (a sharp English type or one of the excellent French imports) and freshly grated horseradish for people who prefer something sharper than the customary pickle condiments.

Cheese Hamburgers

1 pound ground beef	1 onion, grated
½ cup grated sharp Cheddar cheese	Salt and freshly ground pepper to taste
1 tablespoon Worcestershire sauce	4 strips bacon

Mix all ingredients, except bacon, and form into four patties. Wrap each patty with a slice of bacon and grill as Plain Hamburgers (opposite) to desired degree of doneness.

To serve: These are exceptionally good topped with sliced raw onion marinated in an olive oil and wine vinegar dressing with plenty of hot mustard.

Serves 2.

Savory Hamburgers

1 pound ground beef	1 tablespoon mushroom powder
1 medium onion, minced	Salt and freshly ground pepper to taste
½ cup chopped ripe olives	

Mix all ingredients, except the salt and pepper, and form into four patties. Grill as Plain Hamburgers (opposite), seasoning with salt and pepper as the meat cooks.

To serve: Accompany these hamburgers with crisp fried potatoes and a salad of sliced tomatoes dressed with olive oil and wine vinegar and garnished with black olives and strips of anchovies.

Serves 2.

Beefsteak Bismarck

2 pounds ground beef	1 teaspoon salt
2 tablespoons butter, melted	2 teaspoons freshly ground pepper
¼ cup lightly chopped green onions	4 soft-fried eggs

Lightly mix the ground beef with the butter, green onions, salt, and pepper. Form into four patties and grill as Plain Hamburgers (opposite) to desired degree of doneness.

To serve: Top each hamburger with a soft-fried egg and for accompaniments have plain boiled potatoes liberally dressed with butter and chopped parsley, tomatoes broiled with a seasoning of chopped garlic and basil, and plenty of cold ale.

Serves 4.

Herbed Hamburgers

1 pound ground beef	1 egg, lightly beaten
¼ cup chopped chives	Salt and freshly ground pepper to taste
¼ cup chopped parsley	
2 teaspoons rosemary	

Mix all ingredients well and form into four patties. Grill as Plain Hamburgers (page 31) to desired degree of doneness.

To serve: Present the hamburgers on heated buns.

Serves 2.

Mexican Hamburgers

1 pound ground beef	1 tablespoon chili powder
1 small green pepper, chopped	1 tablespoon chili sauce
1 medium onion, chopped	Salt and freshly ground pepper to taste

Mix all ingredients well and form into four patties. Grill as Plain Hamburgers (page 31) to desired degree of doneness.

Serves 2.

Hamburger and Eggplant

8 small, thin slices eggplant	1 small onion, grated
Seasoned flour for dredging	1 small clove garlic, grated
1 pound ground beef	Salt and freshly ground pepper to taste

Dredge the eggplant slices in seasoned flour and grill lightly, just until they are brown and tender. Keep them hot. Mix the ground beef with the onion, garlic, and salt and pepper. Form into eight patties about the size of the eggplant slices. Grill quickly to desired degree of doneness.

To serve: Place each of four patties between two slices of eggplant and top with the remaining patties. Present them with your favorite barbecue or tomato sauce poured over each serving.

Serves 4.

Hamburger Cheese Sandwich

Arrange two thin patties of hamburger sandwich-fashion with blue cheese spread between. Wrap with strip of bacon around the rim, secure with toothpicks, and broil until the bacon crisps and the cheese oozes.

Hamburger Rarebit

Cover hamburger patties with your favorite welsh rarebit recipe, which may be prepared in the electric skillet beside your grill.

Corned Beefburgers

Here's a tasty change from the usual hamburger fare. Use a good brand of canned corned beef hash or—much better—make your own mixture.

4 cups chopped corned beef	Pinch of nutmeg
2 cups cubed lightly boiled potatoes	Salt and freshly ground pepper to taste
1 or 2 onions, chopped	4 poached eggs

Mix all ingredients well, except the eggs, and form into four patties. Brush with melted butter and grill over hot coals or in a hot skillet. Cook slowly until the patties are crusty and brown on the outside.

To serve: Top each patty with a poached egg and a tart sauce, such as a chili sauce.

Serves 4.

Mexican Corned Beefburgers

To the corned beef mixture add 4 tablespoons of chili sauce and 1 very finely chopped green pepper.

Broiled Chickenburgers

Chickenburgers are a real treat. They take a bit of preparing, but the results are well worth it.

1 chicken or fowl (4 to 5 pounds), giblets reserved	1 teaspoon rosemary or tarragon
Salt and freshly ground pepper to taste	2 eggs, lightly beaten
	Dry toast crumbs
	4 to 6 strips bacon
	Melted butter

Strip all the flesh from the chicken. Cut the skin and tendons away and put the meat and reserved giblets through the medium blade of a meat chopper. To the ground meat add the salt and pepper, rosemary, eggs, and enough crumbs to bind the whole together. Form into flat patties and wrap a strip of bacon around the rim of each patty, securing it with toothpicks. Brush with melted butter and grill slowly until the patties are nicely browned and cooked through.

Serves 4 to 6.

Pan-Broiled Chickenburgers

Prepare as Chickenburgers (above) and pan-broil slowly in butter. Make the following sauce after the patties are cooked: To the pan add a little flour and blend with the butter in the pan. Gradually stir in 1 cup of heavy cream and keep stirring until it thickens. Taste for seasoning and add a little freshly ground pepper. Pour over the chickenburgers and garnish with chopped parsley.

Serves 4 to 6.

Lamburgers

1 pound ground lean lamb (shoulder or leg)	¼ cup chopped parsley Salt and freshly ground pepper to taste
1 small onion, chopped	4 strips bacon
1 clove garlic, grated	Melted butter
1 egg, lightly beaten	

Mix all ingredients, except bacon and butter, well. Form into four flat patties and surround each patty with a strip of bacon. Brush with melted butter. Grill as Plain Hamburgers (page 31), or pan-broil them. You will find that lamburgers are juicier if they are rare in the middle.

Serves 2.

Helen Brown's Heartburgers

Clean a beef heart and put it through a meat chopper. Season with salt and freshly ground pepper and form into patties. Brush on the grill as you would hamburgers.

To serve: Leave the heartburgers in the foil and accompany with potatoes cooked in the ashes and quantities of butter.

Franks

Most Americans think they know all there is to know about cooking frankfurters. They simply grill them in a pan or on a folding grill (or, heaven forbid, boil them), slap them on a tasteless frankfurter roll, pass the mustard and piccalilli, and that's it. Actually the lowly hot dog is a very versatile animal if properly treated, and can be distinctive eating.

First of all, if you're going to serve them sandwich fashion, don't feel bound to use the standard frankfurter roll. Try instead some tender little finger rolls from your local bakery or, better yet, some small French rolls. You'll find either of these finer in texture and better flavored than the mass-produced standby.

Try some of the following suggestions for sprucing up the hot dog.

Cheese-stuffed franks: Cut a deep slit in one side of each frankfurter, insert some sharp Cheddar cheese, and wrap the frankfurter with a strip of bacon to hold it together. Fasten with a toothpick and grill.

Chili franks: Grill whole frankfurters and serve with homemade chili.

Franks and tomatoes: Pan-broil thick slices of beefsteak tomatoes, grill frankfurters, and serve each one on top of a tomato slice.

Cocktail franks: Heat frankfurters or knockwurst over hot coals. Cut them into bite-sized pieces, insert a toothpick in each one, and serve with a large bowl of hot barbecue sauce for guests to dunk their portions into. This is good as a hot snack with drinks.

Cheesefurters: Grill frankfurters, place on toasted rolls, top with pickle relish and a slice of cheese. Reheat to melt the cheese.

Texas hots: Serve grilled franks on toasted rolls and heap ground meat and chili and chopped raw onion in the sandwich.

Barbecued franks: Put grilled franks on hot toasted buttered rolls, add some good barbecue sauce, and heat.

Sauced franks: Sauté chopped onion in butter until just soft. Add tomato sauce, season to taste with salt and freshly ground pepper, and bring to a bubbling boil. Add dairy sour cream to taste, cook until just hot but not boiling. Top frankfurter sandwiches with this sauce.

French franks: Spread a French roll with garlic butter to which you have added some chopped chives and parsley; add a grilled frankfurter and a slice of cheese. Wrap the whole thing in a piece of foil and heat until the cheese melts. Have a bowl of hot barbecue sauce handy for everyone to dunk his serving in.

Long frankfurter roll: Split a loaf of French bread

the long way, butter it with garlic butter, and toast lightly. On the bottom half arrange sliced tomatoes, sliced onions, sliced cucumbers, frankfurters or knockwurst which have been split and grilled, and mayonnaise. Add cheese if you like. Top with the other half of the loaf. Cut through in thick slices the round way. Serve with radishes and green onions.

Liverwurst Franks

12 frankfurters or 6 knockwurst
½ pound liverwurst
2 tablespoons grated onion

½ cup dairy sour cream
Dash of Tabasco sauce
Prepared mustard

Slice the frankfurters down the middle. Mash the liverwurst and combine it with the onion, sour cream, and Tabasco. Stuff the frankfurters with this mixture and brush with mustard. Wrap in foil, two frankfurters to each package. Cook in the foil on the grill for 12 to 15 minutes, turning them twice during the process.

Serves 6.

LAMB

There is a great difference between real spring lamb and yearling lamb. The latter more nearly resembles good mutton. True spring lamb is hard to find. Check with your butcher and see what he can do for you.

Lamb Steaks

Lamb steak is cut from the leg. It should be about 1 inch thick. If good mutton is available in your neighborhood, it's even better for steak. Grill slowly, turning often, and season to taste just before serving. Be sure to serve it on piping-hot plates. If you like the flavor of tarragon, sprinkle a little on the steaks as they grill. Or press rosemary into both sides of the steak and grill.

For lamb steaks, you may have to buy a whole leg and ask your butcher to cut you some slices off the meaty end. (You can use the shank end to braise with lentils for another meal.) You should get four to five good-sized steaks from the average leg. If this seems too extravagant, have a shoulder of lamb boned and rolled and then cut into slices for steaks.

Mutton may be treated in the same way, but be sure to cut away the excess fat that comes on it.

Lamb Steaks in Curry Marinade

1 clove garlic, crushed	¾ cup soy sauce
1 tablespoon curry powder	Lamb steaks
Dash of ginger	

Combine all ingredients and marinate the steaks in this for 1 hour before grilling.

Makes ¾ cup marinade.

Lamb Chops

Lamb chops are no good at all if they are not cut thick, and by thick I mean anywhere from 1½ to 3 inches in thickness. Lamb chops should be of U.S. Prime or U.S. Choice meat. If you are going to grill the chops, don't try to take economical short cuts. I think a loin chop is the only cut for the outdoor grill. Rib chops are just a little delicate for this type of treatment unless a rack of 3 or 4 small chops is cooked for each person. This, of course, means extra work.

Serve lamb chops pink and rare on hot plates. The hot plate is especially important with lamb, as its grease is distasteful if cold. Serve big thick chops with baked potatoes.

Broiled Lamb Chops

To be perfectly cooked, a loin lamb chop should be well browned and crispy on the outside. The fat should be crisp and well done and the center should be pink in color. Start the chops over a medium low fire and turn them once or twice. Test them for doneness by slitting the meat close to the bone to see the degree of pinkness they have reached. Just as with steak, if you want them very charred, you may bring up the heat for the last few moments. A 2- to 2½-inch lamb chop should take about 12 to 14 minutes to broil.

Tarragon-Broiled Lamb Chops

Cream together 4 tablespoons of butter and 2 teaspoons dried tarragon which has been soaked for 30 minutes in 2 tablespoons of white wine or vermouth. Make small incisions in the fat side of the lamb chops with a sharp knife and stuff bits of the tarragon butter in each chop. Broil and brush with remaining tarragon butter before serving.

Saddle Lamb Chops

For centuries the English has been cutting thick lamb chops right across the saddle, thus giving each person two loin chops joined together. These should be cut about 2 inches thick; and if you wish, a kidney may be rolled into the side of each one, although it is my belief that the kidney cooks too much when prepared this way. Tie a strip of rather lean bacon around each chop and broil slowly.

To serve: Saddle lamb chops are wonderfully good with potatoes baked in the ashes and accompanied by an excellent cole slaw. Or, serve with crisp sautéed potatoes and unadorned watercress. They are so good themselves that they need no saucing.

Serves 2.

Mushroom-Stuffed Lamb Chops

4 loin lamb chops
(2 inches thick each)
½ pound mushrooms,
finely chopped

6 tablespoons butter
Salt and freshly ground
pepper to taste
1 teaspoon flour

Cut a pocket in each of the chops. In a skillet, sauté the mushrooms in the butter for 30 minutes over low heat. Season to taste with salt and pepper and just before removing from the heat, stir in the flour and allow it to cook until the mixture is slightly thickened.

Stuff the pockets of the chops with the mushroom mixture and secure the chops with small skewers, either wood or metal. Broil the chops according to the directions for Broiled Lamb Chops (page 41).

Serves 4.

Garlic-Stuffed Lamb Chops

Lamb and garlic have always had an affinity for each other.

6 loin lamb chops
(2½ inches thick each)
2 cloves garlic

3 tablespoons olive oil
2 teaspoons chopped
parsley

Cut a pocket in each of the chops. Crush the garlic and finely chop or press it. Combine the chopped garlic with the olive oil and parsley.

Add a spoonful of the mixture to the pocket of each chop. Press closed; these do not have to be skewered. Broil the chops according to directions for Broiled Lamb Chops (page 41) and brush with additional garlic sauce.

Serves 6.

Mutton Chops

Mutton is a word that is almost taboo in America; yet I am certain if you find good American or Canadian mutton, have the chops cut thick, and grill them properly, you will be delighted with the results. Broiled mutton chops, to be at their best, should be cut very thick, 2 to 3 inches. If you like the taste of garlic, rub well with a bud and grill them over a fairly slow to medium heat, as you would lamb chops. During part of the procedure I always turn them on the fat side so that the large amount of fat, which is normal in good mutton, has a chance to try out. As with lamb, you will have a better dish if you serve them on the rare side.

To serve: Mutton must be presented on very hot plates or the fat will congeal and make a most unattractive service.

English Mutton Chops

Like the English cut of lamb chop, these are usually cut across the saddle. However, one New York restaurant which is famous for its mutton chops cuts them from the rack, about three ribs to a chop. In either case the chops should be grilled on three sides and should be served according to your preferred state of doneness.

To serve: I feel that cole slaw (pages 190–191) and baked potatoes are a must, as well as good ale or beer.

HAM AND PORK

Both precooked and fresh ham make excellent grilled steaks and are good choices to vary your menu.

Ham Steak

The best steaks come from old-fashioned smoked ham. I feel that good ham steak should be from 1½ to 2½ inches thick for grilling over the coals. It should be grilled slowly over a low heat so that it cooks without charring too much. Its own fat will provide the crispy outside that it needs to be delicious. A ham steak between 1½ and 2½ inches will need between 40 and 60 minutes of grill time to make it thoroughly tender and well cooked.

Glazed Ham Steak

Grill ham steak as above. When it is three-fourths cooked, combine with a mixture of ½ cup of honey, the juice of 1 lemon, and 2 teaspoons (more or less) of dry mustard.

Marinated Ham Steak

Marinate a ham steak in enough pineapple juice to cover. Add ¼ cup of sherry, 1 teaspoon of dry mustard, and a few dashes of Worcestershire sauce. Grill the ham steak as above, basting several times during the cooking.

Barbecued Ham Steak

1 ham steak (1½ to 2 inches thick)	3 tablespoons brown sugar
1 tablespoon dry mustard	Few drops of lemon juice
3 tablespoons chili sauce	½ cup dry red wine

Score the fat on the outside of the ham. Combine the remaining ingredients. Grill according to direction for Ham Steak (page 44), basting with the wine mixture while it cooks.

Makes about ¾ cup basting sauce.

Pan-Broiled Ham Steaks

For pan-broiling have the steaks cut a little thinner—about ½ inch thick will do. Grease the pan with some of the ham fat and cook the steaks slowly until they are well browned on both sides.

To serve: Apple rings, browned in the ham fat, are an excellent accompaniment.

Pork Steak

The French do this to perfection, although it is a much neglected dish in this country. The steaks are cut from the fresh ham, as it is called in the East, or the leg, as it is called in the West—and should be between 1½ and 2 inches thick.. Pork steak must be cooked slowly and well. Rub it with a little butter or melted pork fat before placing it on a grill over a fairly slow fire. Turn it over and cook until it is nicely browned, tender, and cooked through. Salt and pepper it well and serve with Devil Sauce (page 198).

Oriental Pork Steaks

1 large onion, finely chopped	Dash of whiskey
½ to ¾ cup soy sauce	Pork steaks (1½ to
1 teaspoon chopped gingerroot	2 inches thick each)

Combine all ingredients except the pork steaks. Let the steaks stand in this marinade for several hours before cooking. Turn the steaks frequently. Grill over slow heat, turning often and basting with the marinade.

Makes ½ to ¾ cup marinade.

Variations

● Crush a clove of garlic, add ½ to ¾ cup of soy sauce, and 1 teaspoon dry mustard. Proceed as above.
● To 3 tablespoons of sesame seeds, add 2 tablespoons of olive oil, 1 tablespoon of chili powder, and ¾ cup of tomato juice. Salt to taste. Proceed as above.

Pan-Broiled Pork Steaks

Grease the pan lightly with a little of the fat from the pork. Season the steaks with salt, freshly ground pepper, and any one of the following herbs—thyme, basil, oregano, or rosemary. Brown them slowly on one side and then turn to brown on the other. Continue cooking until the meat is thoroughly done. This will take from 30 to 45 minutes.

To serve: Sliced onion may be browned in the pork fat and served with the steaks. Or, core tart apples, leaving the skin on, cut them in slices, and brown in the pork fat.

Garlic-Marinated Pork Steaks

1 clove garlic, crushed	Pork steaks (1½ to
½ to ¾ cup soy sauce	2 inches thick each)
1 teaspoon dry mustard	

Combine the garlic, soy sauce, and mustard. Let the steaks stand in this marinade for several hours before cooking. Grill them over slow heat, turning often and basting with the marinade.

Makes ½ to ¾ cup marinade.

Pork Chops

There is one thing to remember when cooking pork: it must be well done. Cook it slowly, a good distance from the coals, and turn it often. It should be thoroughly cooked.

Buy thick chops from the loin—about 1½ inches thick—and allow two chops per person. Cook them slowly, turning often, and season to taste with salt and freshly ground pepper as they cook. Gash the fat before placing the chops on the grill; this helps to melt it down.

Country-Style Pork Chops

Cover pork chops (two to a person) with milk and coarsely ground pepper. Let them marinate in this mixture for several hours. Remove and grill the chops slowly over a medium fire, turning often and allowing the chops to cook for some time on the fat side. Salt them just before serving.

To serve: Make a real old-fashioned cream gravy with the milk in which you marinated the chops. I like to serve home-fried potatoes and broiled apple rings, which should be sprinkled with granulated sugar for the last few minutes of their grilling.

Deviled Pork Chops

Grill thick loin chops according to directions given for Pork Chops (page 47). When they are cooked through and nicely browned, remove each chop and press into buttered crumbs. Return to grill to brown the crumbs. Each chop should have one surface nicely coated with browned crumbs.

To serve: Accompany the chops with Devil Sauce (page 98).

Italian-Style Pork Chops

6 pork loin chops (2½ inches thick each)	½ teaspoon salt
3 cloves garlic, finely chopped	½ cup chopped mush-rooms
1 tablespoon chopped fresh basil or 1½ teaspoons dried sweet basil	¼ cup tomato puree Garlic-flavored olive oil

Cut a slit in each chop to form a pocket. Combine the remaining ingredients, except the garlic-flavored olive oil, and blend. Add a spoonful of this mixture to the pocket in each chop and press closed. Grill slowly, basting with a little of the garlic-flavored olive oil from time to time.

To serve: Buttered noodles topped with Parmesan cheese go well with these chops. You may make additional sauce and cook it for 15 minutes to pour over the cooked chops if you wish.

Serves 6.

Barbecued Pork Chops

Marinate pork chops in Pungent Barbecue Sauce (page 201). Let them stand for an hour or so in the mixture and baste them with the sauce during the grilling.

Pan-Broiled Pork Chops

Pork chops may be pan-broiled as you would pork steaks. Simply brown them quickly on both sides and then continue cooking slowly until thoroughly done. Season to taste with salt and pepper.

To serve: These chops go well with grilled onions or apple rings browned in the pork fat.

Braised Pork Chops

Brown quickly in a hot pan and cover with a barbecue sauce of your choice. Place a lid on the pan and cook slowly until the chops are tender.

Pork Chops with Sauerkraut

Brown the chops quickly in a hot pan and cover with sauerkraut. Place a lid on the pan and simmer slowly until the meat is tender.

Pork Tenderloin

Pork tenderloins are extremely popular in some areas and very difficult to find in other parts of the country. If you can find them, they are a delicious morsel brushed with butter and grilled over a medium fire for 15 to 18 minutes. Add a little thyme or basil. Allow one tenderloin per person.

Grilled Pigs' Feet

This unusual dish is simple to prepare at the last minute if the pigs' feet have already been cooked and stored in the refrigerator. When you shop for pigs' feet, look for the long ones. They are not always easy to find. In New York I go to Chinatown to buy them. Allow one per serving.

Wrap each pig's foot in cotton material and tie securely to keep the skin from breaking during the long cooking process. Put them in a large kettle with 2 cloves of garlic, an onion stuck with cloves, a bay leaf, salt, a little vinegar, and water to cover. Bring it to a boil, turn down the heat, and let the kettle simmer for about 5 hours. Remove the pigs' feet, unwrap them, and put them in a bowl. Pour the broth over them and let them chill.

When you are ready to grill them, dip each one in beaten egg and then roll in crumbs. Grill over charcoal until nicely browned and crusty and heated through.

To serve: Accompany with Devil Sauce (page 198), fried potatoes, and watercress without dressing. You'll find this a truly delicious dish.

Italian Sausage

Sweet and hot Italian sausages are delicious grilled over charcoal. Poach them for 5 to 8 minutes before grilling to cook out excess fat. They then grill quickly and to a delicious brownness. Have both sweet and hot sausages. Serve with crisp Italian bread and, if you wish, a great bowl of green noodles with butter and grated cheese.

VEAL

Veal Steaks

Veal steaks, cut from the leg, should be 1½ to 2 inches thick. They take long, slow cooking. Grill them slowly over moderate heat, basting frequently, and season to taste.

Because veal is lean and dries out easily, it is the least desirable meat for charcoal broiling. Good results are obtained, however, when it is pan-broiled.

Braised Veal Steaks

Season the meat with salt and freshly ground pepper and sprinkle lightly with flour. Have your pan hot and a good amount of butter bubbling in it. Brown the steaks on both sides, reduce the heat, cover the pan, and simmer slowly until the veal is thoroughly done and tender. Add more butter or a little olive oil to prevent sticking or burning.

Braised Veal Pepper Steak

1 clove garlic, crushed	Salt and freshly ground
3 tablespoons olive oil	pepper to taste
1 veal steak	Flour
(1½ to 2 inches thick)	2 green peppers,
	cut in strips

Sauté the garlic in olive oil. Season the steak with salt and pepper and sprinkle with a little flour. Brown it on both sides in the oil and place the green pepper strips over the meat. Cover the pan and simmer until the veal is tender.

Veal Steak with Wine Sauce

1 veal steak (1½ to	Butter
2 inches thick)	2 to 3 tomatoes, peeled
Salt and freshly	and finely chopped
ground pepper to taste	1½ teaspoons basil
Flour	½ cup red or white wine

Season the meat with salt and pepper and sprinkle lightly with flour. Cook in butter according to directions for Braised Veal Steaks (above). When the meat is tender, remove it to a hot platter.

Add the tomatoes, basil, and wine to the pan. Let it all boil up and blend thoroughly. Taste for seasoning and pour over the meat.

Serves 2.

Veal Chops

Veal chops are the least desirable meat for a charcoal grill. They are, however, good when larded, marinated, or braised. They should be cut 1½ to 2 inches thick and grilled slowly. Baste from time to time with bacon fat or butter. Salt and pepper to taste.

Veal is improved by the addition of some extra seasoning. Try serving the chops with a good barbecue sauce (pages 199–204) to pep them up.

Stuffed Veal Chops

6 loin veal chops (2 to 2½ inches thick each)
¼ pound butter
1 teaspoon chopped chives
1 tablespoon finely chopped parsley
1 tablespoon chopped fresh tarragon or 1 teaspoon dried tarragon

6 strips bacon
Melted bacon fat or butter
Salt and freshly ground pepper to taste

Cut a slit in each chop to form a pocket. Cream the ¼ pound butter with the chives, parsley, and tarragon. Put a spoonful of this mixture in each pocket and bard with a strip of bacon. Secure the bacon and pocket opening of each chop with a skewer. Broil slowly, brushing with melted bacon or butter. Salt and pepper to taste.

Serves 6.

Farm-Style Veal Chops

6 veal chops (2 to 2½ inches thick each)
1 large onion, thinly sliced
2 cups milk

Old-Fashioned Cream Gravy (below)
Melted butter

Put the veal chops with the onion in a flat pan and cover with the milk. Marinate the chops for 3 to 4 hours, turning frequently. Remove the chops from the marinade, reserving the milk and onion, and grill over medium coals, turning repeatedly and brushing with the melted butter.

To serve: Accompany the chops with Old-Fashioned Cream Gravy (below) and tiny new potatoes boiled in their jackets.

Old-Fashioned Cream Gravy

Sliced onion reserved from marinade (above)
4 tablespoons butter
3 tablespoons flour

Milk reserved from marinade (above)
Salt and freshly ground pepper to taste

Sauté the sliced onion in the butter until it is soft and lightly browned. Add the flour and when this is well blended and lightly browned, gradually stir in the milk and continue stirring until the gravy thickens. Season to taste with salt and pepper.

Makes 2 cups gravy.

Braised Deviled Veal Chops

Dip veal chops in beaten egg and then in seasoned bread crumbs. Brown in a hot pan with plenty of melted butter. When browned on both sides, place a cover on the pan and simmer the chops slowly until tender and well done. Serve with Devil Sauce (page 198).

VARIETY MEATS

Liver, whole or sliced, kidneys, and heart all lend themselves to charcoal grilling and are particularly delicious eating. If you're a hunter and bag a deer or two, you may apply the rules for calf's liver to deer liver and find it a rare treat. Since all variety meats are perishable, it is better to grill them in the garden rather than to transport them long distances. They usually are enhanced by a sharp sauce.

Liver

Broiled Liver Steaks

Calf's liver, good lamb liver, and, at times, baby beef liver are all excellent for liver steaks. These should be cut 1 to 3 inches thick and should be fresh, not frozen, liver.

Butter the slices and broil quickly over a moderate fire, charring well on the outside and cooking the inside to your preferred state of rareness. I believe that liver is much more delicious when well charred and quite pink in the center.

To serve: Liver steak with a béarnaise sauce or with garlic butter is excellent. A huge bowl of thickly sliced tomatoes and sliced raw onions makes a fine accompaniment.

Pan-Broiled Liver Steak

1	liver steak (1 inch thick)	1	medium onion, chopped
	Seasoned flour	1/3	cup dry white wine
3	tablespoons butter	1/2	cup dairy sour cream

Dredge the steak with flour. Melt 2 tablespoons of the

butter in a skillet until it is sizzling and pop the steak in. Cook until crusty on one side and then turn to brown the other side. Remove the steak to a hot platter and keep it warm.

Add the remaining tablespoon of butter and the onion to the pan. Cook just until the onion begins to get soft. Add the wine and cook it up for a bit. Lower the heat and add the sour cream. Blend and heat thoroughly, but do not let the mixture come to a boil. Pour over the steak and serve.

Serves 1.

Stuffed Liver Rolls

Have the butcher cut thin slices of liver and cover each one with a thin slice of ham—preferably Italian proscuitto. Roll the liver slices around the prosciutto and secure with small skewers or toothpicks. Brush well with melted butter and grill over moderate coals, turning several times during the grilling. The liver should be pinky rare and the ham just heated through.

Kidneys

The only kidneys that are palatable to me for outdoor grilling are veal kidneys and lamb kidneys. You will find lamb kidneys in the skewer-cookery section.

Broiled Veal Kidneys

You may leave some of the fat on veal kidneys if you wish—in fact, for charcoal grilling, I find it is wiser to do so. Allow 1 kidney per person. Either split the kidneys or cut them in 3 slices, depending on the size. Remove the cores, and if you prefer mild-flavored kidneys, soak them in milk for an hour. (Veal kidneys, in my opinion, do not need this.) Brush the kidneys with melted butter or olive oil and grill them very quickly, since overcooked kidneys are always tough.

Kidneys should be pleasantly browned on the outside. Salt and pepper them before serving.

To serve: I like kidneys with olive butter and sautéed potatoes.

Deviled Veal Kidneys

Slice kidneys, 1 to a person, in 3 slices, keeping some of the fat on them. Broil as above and just before they are done, roll in fried bread crumbs and return to the grill to brown very quickly.

To serve: Devil Sauce (page 198) is a fine accompaniment.

Heart

For four people you will need 8 lamb hearts, 4 veal hearts, or 1 beef heart. (Since size varies, you might prefer to allow ½ pound per person.)

Broiled Heart

2 lamb hearts or 1 veal heart	2 cloves garlic, finely chopped
1 teaspoon salt	1 teaspoon rosemary
1 teaspoon freshly ground pepper	Olive oil
1 medium onion, thinly sliced	

Clean and split the heart or hearts. Put in a bowl, sprinkle with the remaining ingredients, except the olive oil, and marinate for 1 hour. Brush well with olive oil and grill quickly so that you get a pleasantly charred surface on the outside and a nice pinkness on the inside.

To serve: Garlic butter and rice pilaf are fine accompaniments to this dish.

Serves 1.

POULTRY

The various birds classified as poultry take easily to the barbecue or grill. They should be split carefully, and the backbone or spinal column should be removed completely so that the *halves* roast easily on the grill. It is my belief that halved birds cook best if they are brushed liberally with butter, oil, or a favorite sauce and placed on the grill bone-side-down. About halfway through the broiling process, turn the skin side to the heat and continue the broiling. If the birds are not moist or fat, it is a good idea to brush or baste them with butter, oil, or sauce as they cook.

Small birds, such as squab or squab chicken, may be broiled whole with four or five turns during the broiling period. Larger birds, such as capon and turkey, may be halved or quartered for the broiling period and the same technique followed.

Parts of chickens or turkeys may be broiled. It is my feeling that they should be cooked in a basket type of grill. Serve broiled poultry right from the grill, when it is at its crisp, delicious best.

Chicken

Broiled Chicken

Have the butcher split your chickens for broiling and remove the backbone and the end part of the breastbone. This makes them lie much flatter on the grill. Rub the meat well with butter, salt, pepper, and paprika. Grill bone-side-down. Turn once during the broiling to give the skin time to brown and crisp. Baste with melted butter. For a change, combine lemon juice and melted butter in equal quantities. Chicken will take from 25 to 45 minutes, according to size. They are delicious served with sautéed (page 174) or home fried (page 175) potatoes.

Rosemary-Broiled Chicken

Prepare chickens as above and broil bone-side-down. Before turning, dip the chickens into melted butter and press them into fresh rosemary leaves, turn, and broil. When the broiling is finished, bring up the fire so that the leaves will char, imparting a fine scent of the herb.

Oriental Chicken

2 broiler-fryer chickens, halved	2 tablespoons grated gingerroot or 1 teaspoon ginger
1 cup soy sauce	
1 cup sherry	Sesame seeds

Marinate the chicken halves in the soy sauce, sherry, and gingerroot for 1 hour. Grill bone-side-down. Turn once during the broiling to give the skin time to brown and crisp. Baste with a little of the marinade from time to time.

Just before the chickens are ready to serve, remove them from the grill and press the skin side into the sesame seeds. Return to the grill so that the seeds can toast.

Serves 4.

Marinated Broilers

Make a marinade with 2 parts olive oil to 1 part dry white wine. Add 1 chopped onion, 1 crushed clove of garlic, and tarragon, salt, and freshly ground pepper to taste. Soak broiler halves in this mixture for 2 to 3 hours. Broil as above, bone-side-down, over white coals. Turn halfway through the cooking and grill skin-side-down. The chickens will take from 25 to 45 minutes to cook, depending on their size.

Sautéed Chicken

Sautéed chicken is an excellent addition to the repertoire of any outdoor cook. By using imagination in changing the seasonings and sauces, the clever cook can create many "specialties" from this basic recipe.

Use broilers cut in quarters or small fryers cut in serving pieces. Have a large skillet with plenty of fat or oil bubbling in it. Use butter, bacon fat, olive or other cooking oil. If you use butter, it's a good idea to use part oil, which will keep the butter from burning. Sprinkle the chicken lightly with seasoned flour and brown each piece on all sides in the grease. When all the chicken is evenly browned, place a lid on the skillet and continue cooking slowly until the chicken is tender. This should take about 20 to 25 minutes. Just before the chicken is done, sprinkle it with chopped parsley.

Variations

● Add onion rings to the pan after the chicken is browned and let them simmer with the chicken pieces.
● Add a green pepper cut in strips to the chicken after it has browned and let them cook down with the chicken. Just before the meat is tender add a handful of chopped chives and parsley.
● Add 1 chopped onion and 1 crushed clove of garlic to the chicken after it is browned. Simmer for 5 minutes. Add 2 or 3 good-sized tomatoes, peeled, seeded, and chopped, and a teaspoon of dried basil.
● Add ½ cup of chopped mushrooms to the chicken and let simmer with the chicken pieces. Just before the chicken is done add ½ cup of heavy cream. When the chicken is tender, arrange the pieces on a hot platter, taste the sauce for seasoning, and pour over the chicken.

Chicken Sauté with White Wine

Use quartered broilers or small fryers cut in serving pieces and brown them in hot grease. When all the pieces are browned, season to taste with salt and freshly ground pepper, and sprinkle with dried tarragon and chopped chives. Pour ½ cup of dry white wine over the chicken, place a cover on the pan, and let it simmer until the chicken is tender.

Chicken Sauté with Chili

Dredge quartered broilers or small fryers cut in serving pieces in flour. Sauté until brown in hot grease. Season to taste with salt and freshly ground pepper; add a dash of cayenne, a crushed clove of garlic, and 1 onion, chopped. Cover and simmer for a few minutes. Add ¾ cup of tomato puree, 2 teaspoons of chili powder, and a pinch of dried basil. Cover again and simmer until the chicken is tender. Remove the chicken pieces to a hot platter, thin the sauce down a little with dry red wine, and pour it over the chicken.

Campfire Fried Chicken

Have fryers cut into serving pieces. Dredge each piece with flour. Heat fat or oil in a large skillet. You will need plenty of fat, about 1 to 1½ inches in depth. (A good idea is to fry several rashers of bacon, set the bacon aside to keep warm, and use the bacon fat to fry the chicken. Then garnish the platter with the bacon.) Have the fat hot but not boiling. Brown each piece of chicken thoroughly. Season to taste, cover, and simmer until done. This should take 20 to 30 minutes, depending on the size of the chicken.

When the chicken is tender, remove it to a hot platter. Skim off all but about 4 tablespoons of fat. Add 3 or 4 tablespoons of flour, blending it in and stirring all around the bottom and sides of the pan to scrap up any pieces of meat or skin that are sticking there. Slowly add 2 cups of half-and-half cream, stirring constantly until smooth and thickened. Taste for seasoning.

To serve: Pass the chicken and sauce separately.

Turkey

Turkeys weighing 4 to 7 pounds will be excellent broiled. They must be split and cooked over low heat —far from the coals—for the first 40 minutes. Then they may be moved closer to the heat to finish cooking and browning.

Grilled Turkey I

Arrange a 4- to 5-pound turkey, halved, bone-side-down on the grill and cook slowly for 25 minutes. Season to taste and turn skin-side-down. Continue cooking for 15 to 20 minutes, or until almost done. To finish cooking, bring meat close to the coals to brown. Baste during the cooking with a little seasoned oil.

Serves 4.

Grilled Turkey II

Buy a 4- to 5-pound turkey broiler and have it split. Cook 1 pound of sliced bacon until it is crisp. Remove from pan and reserve bacon grease, adding to it salt, freshly ground pepper, and paprika. Keep the fat warm. Spread the bone side of the turkey halves with some of the bacon-fat mixture and grill the turkey slowly far from the heat for 25 minutes. Brush the skin side with bacon fat before turning. Brush the turkey twice more with bacon fat as you continue cooking it for 15 to 20 minutes more, until almost done. To finish cooking, bring the meat close to the coals to brown.

To serve: Garnish the broiled turkey with the bacon, tiny green peas cooked with onions and dressed with plenty of butter, and potatoes boiled in their jackets. Follow this with cole slaw as a separate course. Dress the cabbage with a sauce of dairy sour cream and grated horseradish.

Serves 4.

Grilled Turkey Parts

If you are fond of turkey but would rather not have it around for several days, purchase turkey parts and broil them according to rules for Grilled Turkey (page 61). Turkey thighs, if they are very large, may be spitted. They may also be boned, stuffed, rolled, and tied as are the whole turkeys. For those who love dark meat—and there are millions of us—this is indeed a delicious treat.

Turkey Steak

1 frozen turkey breast	Juice of 1 lemon
1 cup olive oil or bland cooking oil	2 tablespoons tarragon
½ cup dry white wine	Salt and freshly ground pepper to taste

Turkey steaks must be cut from a frozen bird. Ask your butcher to saw across right through the breast to make 1-inch steaks. Combine the remaining ingredients and blend well. Soak the turkey slices in this marinade until they have thawed out to room temperature. Cut each slice in half and grill slowly over medium heat, basting with the marinade and turning frequently. Allow 20 to 25 minutes a side. Be careful not to overcook the steaks.

DUCK

Broiled Duckling

With broiled duckling, many people miss the pleasure of eating crisply broiled halved ducklings, such as small-sized Long Island ducks. Have the butcher split them or split them yourself. Allow half a duck per person. Season with salt and freshly ground pepper and broil bone-side-down for about 20 to 25 minutes.

Turn for 10 minutes and then return to bone side. The process will take from 45 to 55 minutes. Don't forget to increase the heat at the end of the broiling period to crisp the outside skin.

To serve: Rice, applesauce, and a crisp green salad go well with broiled duckling.

Broiled Duckling with Olives

2 ducklings (4 pounds each)
½ cup chopped stuffed olives
½ teaspoon freshly ground pepper
2 tablespoons butter, softened

Halve the ducklings. Combine the olives, pepper, and butter. Force this mixture under the skin of the ducklings and broil as above.

Serves 4.

Broiled Curried Duckling

2 ducklings (4 pounds each)
1 tablespoon butter
1 tablespoon cooking oil
2 tablespoons finely chopped onion
1½ tablespoons curry powder
¼ cup vermouth or sherry
½ cup honey
Juice of 2 lemons

Have the butcher split the ducklings. Heat the butter and oil in a skillet and sauté the onion until soft. Add the curry powder and vermouth and let simmer for 5 minutes. Add the honey and lemon juice and mix well.

Grill the ducklings according to the directions for Broiled Duckling (pages 62–63) and brush with the curry mixture several times while they cook.

Serves 4.

Savory Broiled Duckling

1 duckling (5 to 6 pounds)	1 teaspoon Kitchen Bouquet
1 tablespoon honey	1 teaspoon soy sauce
	2 tablespoons sherry

Wash the duckling in cold water and dry carefully. Cut in quarters and remove the neck, backbone, and wing tips. Place the duck quarters, skin-side-up, on a broiling rack 15 to 18 inches above glowing coals. The heat should continue steadily for 30 minutes. After 15 minutes, turn the duck quarters skin-side-down. Cook 15 more minutes. Mix the remaining ingredients and blend well. About 5 minutes before the duck is done, brush it all over with this sauce. Continue cooking until done and serve.

Serves 4.

Piquant Grilled Duckling

1 duckling (5 to 6 pounds)	2 tablespoons soy sauce
2 tablespoons cooking oil	1 teaspoon rosemary
⅓ cup finely chopped onion	1 teaspoon Kitchen Bouquet
1 clove garlic, minced	1½ teaspoons dry mustard
½ cup honey	1 teaspoon freshly ground pepper
½ cup tomato catsup	
½ cup red wine vinegar	

Prepare and grill the duck following the directions for Savory Broiled Duckling (above).

While the duck is cooking, heat the cooking oil in a large skillet and sauté the onion and garlic until the onion is transparent. Add the remaining ingredients, mix thoroughly, bring to a boil, and simmer 5 minutes.

About 5 minutes before the duck is done, brush it with this sauce and continue cooking until done.

This seasoning sauce will keep in the refrigerator. Store what you don't use on the duck to add zest to other broiled foods.

Serves 4.

Lemon Duckling

Remove the wing-tips from a 5- to 6-pound Long Island duckling. Slit the skin from the neck to the vent along the breastbone with a sharp knife. Pull the layer of skin and fat away from the flesh with your hand, while you cut any connecting tissue with the knife. Leave the flesh intact. After you have skinned the duckling, cut it in quarters, and remove the backbone.

Brush the duck pieces with Kitchen Bouquet. Melt 2 tablespoons of fat in a skillet. Add the duck and brown each piece on all sides very quickly. Sprinkle with 2 tablespoons of minced onion and salt and freshly ground pepper to taste. Cook a few minutes more. Add one 3-ounce can of sliced broiled mushrooms and 1 lemon thinly sliced. Cover and cook over a moderate heat for 30 to 40 minutes, or until the duck is tender.

To serve: When you skin the duck for this or the following recipe, save the skin and put it in the broiler near the heat. Let it cook until brown and crisp (watch the dripping pan—you may have to pour off the fat), turning it to be sure it gets an even crispness. Serve crisp bits of this skin as an appetizer with cocktails. Accompany the duck with hot buttered noodles.

Serves 4.

Marinated Grilled Duckling

1 duckling (5 to 6 pounds)	½ teaspoon salt
	¼ teaspoon onion salt
2 teaspoons lemon juice	½ teaspoon ginger
1 teaspoon Kitchen Bouquet	

Slit the skin of the duckling from the neck to the vent along the breastbone with a sharp knife. Pull the layer of skin and fat away from the flesh with your hand, while you cut any connecting tissue with the knife. Leave the flesh intact. After you have skinned the duckling, cut it in quarters, remove the backbone, and cut the wings off so that the four pieces will be equally thick.

Place the pieces of duck in a bowl and sprinkle with the remaining ingredients. Toss the pieces gently to coat them evenly. Let them marinate for 30 minutes to soak up the seasonings. Place the pieces, bone-side-down, on a broiling rack 15 to 18 inches above glowing coals, at moderate heat. Cook for 15 minutes and turn. Continue cooking for 15 minutes longer.

Serves 4.

NOTE: When you skin the duck, save the skin and prepare as in the previous recipe to serve as an appetizer with cocktails.

GAME

Pheasant

Young pheasant may be broiled in the same way as you broil chicken. Allow a half pheasant for each guest.

Broiled Pheasant

Clean and split the pheasants and butter them well. Pheasant has a tendency to be very dry and must be well lubricated. Baste it frequently during the cooking process, and be careful not to overcook it; 15 minutes to a side should be ample time. Season to taste and serve.

Variation

Lubricate the pheasant with a piece of bacon or salt pork placed over the breast. Remove the bacon or salt pork for the last few minutes of cooking to get a nice brown on the skin.

Pheasant, Pioneer Style

This is simply pheasant cut in serving pieces, dredged in flour, and fried according to the directions for Campfire Fried Chicken (page 60). Be sure to make the milk gravy to serve with it. It was a favorite dish with the pioneers of the Far West in the early days when pheasant was a common dish on their tables.

Partridge

Partridge improves in flavor if it is hung for several days. Allow one bird per serving.

Broiled Partridge

To broil partridge follow the directions for Broiled Pheasant (page 66), allowing 10 minutes on the bone side and 8 to 10 minutes on the skin side after turning.

To serve: Broiled partridge is delicious on toast spread with Pâté of Partridge Giblets (below).

Pâté of Partridge Giblets Put the partridge giblets and an onion stuck with 2 or 3 cloves in water to barely cover. Simmer until tender. Chop the giblets very fine, moisten them with a little melted butter and some of the broth in which they were cooked. Spread this mixture on pieces of toast and arrange the broiled partridge halves on the toast.

Sautéed Partridge

Clean and split as for broiling. Dredge each half with seasoned flour. Chop the giblets fine. Have a large skillet ready and brown three or four strips of bacon in it. When the bacon is crisp, remove it to a hot plate and keep it warm. Brown the partridge in the bacon fat, skin side first. When thoroughly browned, cover and simmer for 10 or 12 minutes. Remove the cover and add the chopped giblets. Cook for 7 or 8 minutes more.

Remove the partridge pieces to a hot platter, sprinkle a little flour in the pan, add 1 cup of heavy cream or dairy sour cream, and stir until heated through and thick. Be sure the sauce does not boil or it will curdle. Taste for seasoning.

To serve: Garnish the partridge with bacon strips.

Quail

Quail, as opposed to most game birds, should be fresh when cooked. They are delicious morsels, so allow at least one bird per serving—more if true gourmands are present.

Broiled Quail

Quail may be broiled according to the directions for Broiled Pheasant (page 66), but will need only about 5 minutes per side when broiled on a very hot grill. Baste constantly.

Quail Sautéed with White Grapes

Clean and split quail as for broiling. Brown quickly in plenty of butter, season to taste with salt and freshly ground pepper, and add ½ cup of broth. (Make the broth by cooking the giblets in a little water with an onion—or use chicken bouillon cubes and hot water.) Cover the pan and let the quail simmer over low heat for 8 to 10 minutes. Remove the cover, add a dash of whiskey and ½ to 1 cup of white seedless grapes. Cover again and simmer until the quail are tender.

Squab

Squab should be very fresh when cooked. One squab per person is usually ample, but if they are small or you have invited hearty eaters you may need two per person.

Broiled Squab

Have the squab cleaned and split for broiling as you do chicken. Rub them well with butter or fat and broil on a moderately hot grill, placing the bone side to the flame. Cook for 8 minutes and turn the skin side to the flame, basting with butter again. Allow 10 to 12 minutes cooking time and test for doneness at the thigh joint. If in doubt, cook a little longer, as squab is one bird it is hard to overcook. Season to taste with salt and freshly ground pepper.

Squab Sautéed with Bacon

Clean and split squab as for broiling. Cook 4 or 5 strips of bacon in a skillet until they are brown and crisp. Remove them to a platter. Brown the squab on all sides in the bacon fat, season to taste, cover the skillet, and simmer for 15 to 20 minutes, or until the birds are done.

Remove the squab to a hot platter, pour off all but 3 tablespoons of bacon fat. Add 3 tablespoons of flour and blend. Add 1½ to 2 cups of half-and-half cream and stir until thickened and smooth. Crumble the bacon into the sauce and taste for seasoning.

To serve: Pass the sauce separately with the squab.

Squad Sautéed with White Wine

Clean and split squab as for broiling. Have a large skillet ready with butter bubbling in it. Brown the squab on all sides, and season to taste with salt and freshly ground pepper. Add 1 medium onion chopped and ½ cup of dry white wine, cover, and simmer over a low flame for 10 to 15 minutes. Uncover and add a generous sprinkling of dried tarragon. Cook slowly, uncovered, for 5 more minutes. Remove the squab to a hot platter, add a little more wine to the pan, and bring the pan juices to a boil.

To serve: Place the squab on warm plates and pass the sauce separately.

WILD DUCK

Broiled Wild Duck

Clean, split, and remove the backbone of the duck. Rub with butter or fat to keep it from drying out during the cooking process. Broil, bone-side-down, over moderate heat for 10 to 12 minutes. Turn and continue cooking, skin-side-down, for another 10 minutes or so. Wild duck is at its best when served rare. Allow one bird per person.

Venison

Venison should be hung from three to four weeks to improve its tenderness and flavor.

Venison Steak

Venison steaks can be cut from either the loin or the leg and should be about 2 inches thick. Grill them quickly over hot coals, turning them often. They should be crispy on the outside but rare in the center. Season to taste with salt and freshly ground pepper and serve with a good pat of butter on each steak.

Venison Steak with Pepper

Crush some whole peppercorns, or use prepared cracked pepper. Press the crushed pepper into a venison steak cut from 1 to 1½ inches thick. Cover the steak with pepper on both sides. Heat some butter—a tablespoon or more—in a pan until it is bubbling. Add the steak and sear it quickly on each side. Continue cooking until crusty on the outside and rare in the center. Season with salt and remove to a hot platter. Rinse the pan with whiskey and pour over the steak.

Marinated Venison Steak

Marinate venison steaks in a mixture of olive oil, lemon juice, whiskey, 1 crushed clove of garlic, peppercorns, and salt to taste. Let them stand for 2 or 3 hours before grilling. Grill as Venison Steak (page 70).

Venison Chops

Cut chops, about 1 inch thick, from the loin. If it was a young animal, the chops can be grilled very quickly over hot coals. Baste with plenty of butter, season to taste with salt and freshly ground pepper as you cook.

Pan-Broiled Venison Chops

Chops from a young animal may be cooked quickly in a hot skillet with plenty of butter or beef suet. Get them well browned on both sides, season to taste, and serve at once.

Venison Chops with Sour Cream

The chops from an older animal are more flavorful if treated to a little dressing up. Brown them in a skillet over a hot flame. Season to taste with salt and pepper and add a good big dash of paprika. Add 1 cup or more of dairy sour cream, cover the pan, and simmer for 10 or 15 minutes.

Bear Steak

Bear meat, like pork, can carry trichinosis, and special precautions must be taken with it. The meat *must* be stored at *zero* temperature for several weeks—at least three weeks—before it is cooked. Steaks can be cut from the loin or the leg. Generally speaking, bear meat is better if marinated for a day or two before cooking. It will be much tastier and more tender, especially if the animal is not as young as it might be. Try soaking it in a mixture of olive oil, red wine, chopped onion, and salt and freshly ground pepper. Then grill as you would venison. If the instructions for storing have been faithfully followed, the steaks may be served rare.

SEAFOOD

Fish

Fishermen and ardent campers are never at a loss to cook their catch. Those to whom outdoor cooking is a new experience will be delighted with what they can do with fish on an outdoor grill. One thing to remember always—fish should not be overcooked. Because of their delicate meat, small fish should be grilled in a hinged grill which makes them easier to handle. Good-sized spatulas or pancake turners are a big help in turning large fish on a grill. Plenty of lemon is a necessity with fish. Good butter and olive oil also make for better results.

Grilled Whole Fish

This method can be used for practically any type of fish. Small fish need a brisker heat than large fish, because of the shorter cooking time. I like to butter or oil the inside of a fish and season it with salt and freshly ground pepper. A few slices of onion or a sprig of dill or tarragon inside the fish before broiling gives it a delicious taste. Thin, thin slices of lemon or even orange are excellent.

Oil your grill or your hinged grill well before you start to cook. I find that if you brown the fish well on both sides and continue cooking, turning often, it will be evenly cooked. If you feel that the fish is too dry, baste with a mixture of olive oil and lemon juice.

Fish is cooked when the flesh flakes easily when you test it with a fork, a skewer, or a toothpick. Small fish will cook in 10 to 15 minutes. Larger fish will take up to an hour to cook.

To serve: Lemon, parsley butter, anchovy butter, hollandaise, or béarnaise sauce are excellent complements.

Fish Flambé

In the Mediterranean countries, fish are grilled and removed to a hot platter or a bed of rock salt covered with herbs. They are then topped with sprigs of dried herbs, usually fennel, dill, rosemary, thyme, or parsley. Two to 3 ounces of cognac are poured over them and ignited. The burning alcohol will light the dried herbs, which will tease the taste buds through the nostrils and impart a subtle, delicious flavor to the fish. This process may be used with any small or large fish.

Grilled Fish Steaks

Fish steaks, especially those from the oilier fish, make delicious charcoal-broiled main courses. I like a steak cut from 1½ to 2 inches thick; and for my favorite fish, I must put salmon first, sturgeon second, swordfish third, halibut fourth. The steak, as well as the grill on which it is cooked, should be oiled, and the coals should be moderate. Total cooking time, allowing for turning the fish over once during the process, should be from 12 to 15 minutes, depending upon the thickness and the texture of the steak. You may brush the fish while it is cooking with hot olive oil or melted butter. Salt, freshly ground pepper, and lemon butter may also be used. Fish may be rolled in crumbs, in chopped almonds, or in sesame seeds during the broiling and returned to the grill.

Marinated Fish Steaks

Marinate fish steaks in olive oil which has been cut with lemon juice and flavored with tarragon, dill, tomato puree, or finely chopped garlic. Broil as Grilled Fish Steaks (page 73).

Foil-Cooked Fish Steaks and Fillets

Fish steaks and fillets may be cooked in foil on top of the grill or in the coals. They are delicious combined with butter and thinly sliced tomatoes and cooked 7 to 10 minutes near the coals; turn them several times.

Pan-Fried Fish and Fillets

Small fish and fillets are excellent pan-fried or sautéed. Clean them, roll them in flour, and pop them into a skillet with plenty of bubbling butter. (Remember to mix a little oil in with the butter.) Or you can use bacon fat. Cook the fish over a medium heat until they are brown, turn them gently, season with salt and freshly ground pepper, and brown on the other side. Test for doneness with a fork. Serve with lemon and melted butter.

Larger fish are better filleted or cut into steaks for pan-frying. Follow the same procedure as for small whole fish.

Variations

● When the fish is done, remove it to a hot platter. Add a handful of chopped parsley to the pan and a lump of butter. Boil it up and pour over the fish. Serve with lemon wedges.

- Remove the fish to a hot platter and add half chopped parsley and half chopped chives to the pan with the butter. Proceed as above.
- Remove the fish to a hot platter. Add chopped parsley, butter, and ¼ cup of dry white wine to the pan and proceed as above.
- Fry 4 or 5 strips of bacon in the skillet. When it is crisp, remove the bacon and pour off some of the fat, leaving the amount necessary to pan-fry the fish. Garnish the fish with the bacon crumbled into small pieces.

Shellfish

Broiled Whole Lobster

Lobster is usually split before broiling, but it is my belief that this results in dry lobster meat, tasteless and tough. Broil the lobster whole over coals, allowing about 15 to 20 minutes cooking time. Turn it to cook evenly. Split it after broiling, remove the intestinal vein and stomach, and serve with plenty of melted butter and lemon quarters.

Broiled Split Lobster

You may split live lobsters and spread them lavishly with softened butter and sprinkle with salt, freshly ground pepper, and paprika. Turn them flesh-side-down for about 3 minutes, then turn, spread on more softened butter and continue grilling. The whole process should take from 15 to 20 minutes, depending on the size of the lobsters.

To serve: I like fried bread crumbs, melted butter and lemon juice, and crisp French fried potatoes (page 174) with my broiled lobster.

Soy-Soaked Broiled Shrimp

Choose the very largest shrimps you can find. Split them through the back with sharp scissors, remove the vein, and wash them thoroughly. Marinate them in equal quantities of soy sauce and vermouth for 2 hours. Remove from the marinade and broil for 3 to 4 minutes on the grill.

To serve: Have a collection of sauces—a garlic and anchovy butter, a highly seasoned mayonnaise, and a rich sherry-flavored tomato sauce. Peel the shrimp with your fingers, drop into your favorite sauce, and eat.

Broiled Shrimp Appetizer

24 jumbo shrimp or 36 medium size shrimp	¼ cup finely chopped parsley
1 cup olive oil	3 tablespoons fresh tarragon or 1 table-
Juice of 3 lemons	spoon dried tarragon
¼ cup soy sauce	

With sharp scissors cut down the back of each shrimp shell and remove the vein. Wash the shrimp thoroughly and place them in a large bowl. Combine the remaining ingredients and pour over the shrimp. Let the shrimp stand in this mixture for 2 hours, tossing them around now and then so that they will be evenly marinated.

When you are ready to cook them, arrange the shrimp in basket grills and cook over hot coals for 5 or 6 minutes, turning twice. They should be tender and moist with slightly charred shells.

Serves 6.

Dill-Soaked Broiled Shrimp

Soak large split shrimp, vein removed, in white wine or dry vermouth to which you have added finely chopped garlic and fresh dill. After 2 hours remove the shrimp from the marinade and broil 3 to 4 minutes.

To serve: Dill-flavored mayonnaise and thinly sliced cucumbers marinated in olive oil, vinegar, salt, and freshly ground pepper are delicious with these shrimp.

Charcoal Baked Oysters

Arrange unopened oysters on the grill above a moderate charcoal fire. It will take anywhere from 6 to 8 minutes for the shells to open. Oysters must not overcook but they must heat through. Any type of restaurant oyster, especially the larger ones from the New Jersey or Delaware coast or the extremely large Pacific oysters, is suitable for this particular treat.

To serve: Melted butter, anchovy butter, tarragon butter, or horseradish-flavored hollandaise are excellent sauces with these oysters. Thin rye bread slices, well buttered, are a perfect accompaniment.

Broiled King Crab Legs

King crab legs may be purchased frozen in many parts of the country. The large legs should be slit in the soft part of the shell. They should be grilled with the split side up. I like to brush them lavishly with a mixture of melted butter, lemon or lime juice, and tarragon and merely heat them through, for they are already cooked before they are frozen.

To serve: They really need, as do most grilled shellfish, French fried potatoes (page 174) and crisp cucumbers for an accompaniment.

GRILLED VEGETABLES

Any combination of vegetables may be cooked in foil, either on the grill or in the ashes. For instance, sliced eggplant, quartered tomatoes, and sliced onions, together with a bit of butter, salt, and freshly ground pepper, may be encased in foil and cooked.

Mushrooms may be cooked in foil with butter.

Canned whole-kernel corn combined with butter, chopped green onions, chopped green pepper, or grated Cheddar cheese may be wrapped in foil and broiled on the grill. It is delicious.

Whole onions or potatoes in their skins may be wrapped in foil and baked in the ashes, as can a great many other vegetables, with wonderful results.

Some vegetables, potatoes in particular, can be more easily prepared in the kitchen than on the grill, especially if you have only one grill. However, if you are camping or picnicking away from home, additional recipes that can be cooked outdoors as well as in the kitchen are in the second section of the book (pages 173–182) and marked with an asterisk (*).

SPIT
ROASTING

Many people consider spitting the only true form of roasting. It is the oldest, although our ancestors, unfortunately, knew nothing of electrically driven spits. We know that the juiciness and evenness of cooking are two of the results most desired from good spit roasting. The flavor imparted by charcoal or wood smoke is one of America's most sought-after gustatory experiences, and any barbecue enthusiast who denies himself the pleasure of spit-roasted meats—especially in these days of easy-to-run attachments—is missing at least half the fun of barbecue cookery.

PREPARING ROASTS FOR THE GRILL

There are certain rules which must be followed if one is going to use modern equipment successfully. Meat must be correctly trussed, tied, and balanced on the spit. If the meat is off center, you stand in danger of ruining your motor and stopping the spit. Furthermore, the meat will be spottily cooked. The meat should not slip around on the spit. The holding forks and, if necessary, additional skewers should be used to ensure its holding firm during the cooking process. Certain meats will shift position while roasting because the fat renders, causing the weight to shift. That is why better grills are equipped with compensators with which to adjust the spit balance during the roasting period. Generally, spitted roasts should be boned and tied. They will be easier to spit and roast more evenly.

ROASTING TEMPERATURES

Roasting temperatures for meat should be about the same as for broiling, if not just a little lower. Additional briquets or pieces of charcoal may be added during the roasting process to obtain a steady temperature on the spit surface. The average spit temperature for roasting is around 300°F. Spits should turn away from the cook, thus enabling the fat to drip on the upward motion of the spit into the dripping pan. Some units are equipped with a special firebox for spitting; but if you do not have such a unit, build your fire toward the back of your grill and put a dripping pan or foil in front of it.

GENERAL RULES FOR ROASTING

Cooking time varies a great deal according to wind, outside temperature, quality of meat, and evenness of cooking temperature. Therefore, I feel it is exceedingly important to use a meat thermometer for good results. Remember that meat continues cooking *after* it is removed from the spit for as much as 30 minutes. As a consequence, when I give a cooked temperature, the meat should be removed at that moment and coasted (held) for 15 to 20 minutes before carving. This gives the juices a chance to set and makes the roast more flavorful and delicious.

If your spit is properly balanced and turns evenly, basting is not necessary. If, however, you wish to impart another flavor or coating to the meat, you'll have to baste it. Too, if the meat is extremely lean, it needs the lubrication that only a good baste can give it. You can use the drippings from the meat or other fat, alone or mixed with wine, or prepare a special basting sauce (see "Sauces and Marinades"). Personally, I prefer a little white wine blended with butter or other fat. I find this gives an excellent finish to most meats.

MEAT

Beef

Any size cut of beef—from the small fillet up to half a steer—can be roasted on a spit, but most rotisserie chefs will find a medium-sized roast best suited to their needs and cooking units.

First of all, remember the rules about buying good beef. You want it aged, well hung, and marbled with fat. It is my opinion that for roasting on a spit the sirloin is a better buy than the prime ribs. The cost may be more, but you will have more edible meat and it will be more tender.

Seasonings

If your roast is the best aged beef and an excellent cut, you need nothing but coarse salt and freshly ground pepper to bring out its fine flavor. However, if you want extra zip, try one of the following three suggestions:

● Rub the meat, flesh and fat both, with dry mustard. Baste with fat from the dripping pan and dry mustard mixed.

● Rub the meat with a little dried or fresh rosemary, or sprinkle it with rosemary seasoning powder. Rosemary and beef have a special affinity.

• Do a roast version of French pepper steak. Press freshly ground black pepper in large quantities into the roast firmly so that it will stick. Baste with the fat and the peppery outside will turn crusty and the flavor of the pepper will permeate the whole roast.

If you are afraid your piece of beef may lack flavor and be a little tough, make a coating of soy sauce, a healthy sprinkling of grated fresh gingerroot, grated garlic, and a little rosemary seasoning powder. Roll the roast around in this and fork some of it into the flesh. Let it stand for a while and when you roast it, baste with some of the fat from the drippings, a little soy sauce, and red wine mixed. Do not salt the roast, as the soy sauce substitutes for salt.

Try any of the marinades suggested on pages 210–213 and baste the roast with the marinade while it is cooking.

Standing Rib Roast

This roast has achieved the greatest popularity of any joint. Roasts of from 2 to 7 ribs may be cooked with ease, for your spit will accompany them. Have the butcher cut them short—a 7-inch cut is very good. Ask him to remove the chine bone and tie the roast securely. Allow 1 pound of trimmed meat for each person. For best results, standing ribs should be spitted on the diagonal and balanced perfectly. Force the spit into the cut side of the meat and diagonally through the length of the roast. (If the meat is not properly balanced on the spit, it will rotate unevenly. Therefore, you must experiment and possibly re-spit the roast several times to achieve perfect balance. Some spits are equipped with a counterweight system that aids in this procedure.) Tighten the screws of the holding forks. Insert your meat thermometer so that it does not touch a bone and roast over a medium fire until the thermometer reads 125°F. (very rare). Coast (hold) on spit or remove from the grill and allow it to stand in a warm place for 15 to 20 minutes before removing the spit and carving. It will take a 5-rib roast, which is my favorite, around 2½ hours to achieve the inner temperature of 125°F. A 2-rib roast is ideal for small family groups and usually takes just over an hour to be perfectly rare.

Rolled Rib Roast

Rolled rib roasts have never been a favorite of mine. Many people prefer them, feeling that they are more easily spitted, although they should also be done on the diagonal. Cooking time is about the same as for a standing rib and the roast should be removed from the heat when it reaches an internal temperature of 125°F. Baste with beef drippings.

Spencer Roast

This is a cut more frequently used on the West Coast than on the East Coast. It is a rib roast with the bone and a good deal of the fat removed. A Spencer may be spitted straight through the roast, or you may spit it as you do a standing rib. It is ideal for roast beef sandwiches. Roast the Spencer to an internal temperature of 125°F. if you want it rare.

Sirloin Roast

This is England's favorite joint for roasting and is occasionally used over here. Known in the eastern part of the country as a boneless strip, it is spitted and roasted like the Spencer and makes delicious eating.

Rump Roast

If your butcher carries U.S. Prime beef, a rolled, barded, and tied rump roast is a very tasty change. Balance it well on the spit—not an easy job because its shape is apt to vary a good deal—and cook to an internal temperature of 125°F.

Whole Roast Tenderloin

A whole tenderloin done on a spit makes a simple and elegant dish, and in spite of the cost per pound at the butcher's, it is really economical, as I pointed out earlier, because it's all solid meat.

Have the butcher roll it in a thin sheet of pounded suet and tie it securely. Salt and freshly ground pepper are all this delicious morsel needs, although I sometimes like to sprinkle it with a little rosemary or rosemary seasoning powder as well. Spit it through the center and roast it about 35 minutes, or until it is nicely crisp on the outside but still rare in the center. It is impossible to give exact cooking time because each cooking unit tends to work a little differently from others.

To serve: When it is done to your satisfaction, remove the tenderloin from the spit and serve it with a béarnaise sauce (pages 208–209) and sautéed potatoes (page 175).

Tenderloin with Red Wine

This is a fancy spitted fillet—the sort of thing you might cook for a very special occasion. Buy a whole fillet and some suet, pounded into a flat, thin sheet, ½ pound of smoked tongue, and some salt pork. Cut the salt pork and the tongue into matchstick-size pieces. With a larding needle prick large holes in the surface of the meat and force pieces of the pork and tongue into these holes. This is called "piquéing" and it adds a great deal to the flavor of a roast. Sprinkle the meat well with freshly ground pepper and add a touch of rosemary or rosemary seasoning powder. Spit the roast and wrap the suet around it lightly for the first 25 minutes of cooking. (Or you can spread it well with fat instead.) Baste it every 10 or 15 minutes with pan drippings mixed with red wine.

To serve: Accompany this fillet with a good green salad and some foil-wrapped potatoes baked in coals or sautéed potatoes (page 175). I like to add a dish

84

of fresh mushrooms cooked in butter and flavored with a little garlic. For this meal a fine red wine is necessary.

Peppered Tenderloin Sandwiches

One of the most practical and delicious foods to serve for an outdoor or buffet party is fillet sandwiches. Buy a whole fillet, or two—according to the number you want to serve. Press coarsely ground pepper or crushed peppercorns (crush them with a rolling pin or use a mortar and pestle) into the meat. Salt it well and sprinkle a little rosemary on it. Spit it and roast until it is done to your satisfaction.

To serve: Cut loaves of French or Italian bread in half the long way, toast lightly, and butter (or use the Herbed Butter, Anchovy Butter, or Mushroom Spread below and next page). Slice the fillets very thin and spread the slices of meat on the bottom halves of the toasted and buttered bread loaves. Top with the upper halves, and cut the long sandwiches into small sections. Serve with potato chips (page 175) slices of ripe tomatoes and red Italian or Bermuda onions.

Herbed Butter

¼ pound butter	½ clove garlic, chopped
½ cup chopped parsley	Salt to taste
¼ cup chopped chives or green onions	

Cream the butter with the remaining ingredients until well blended.

Makes about ¾ cup.

Anchovy Butter

½ pound butter	2 tablespoons chopped parsley
1 can (1¾ ounces) anchovy fillets, including oil, finely chopped	

85

Cream the butter with the remaining ingredients until well blended.

Makes about 1 cup.

Mushroom Spread

4	tablespoons butter	2	tablespoons butter
½	pound mushrooms, finely chopped	¼	cup heavy cream
	Salt and freshly ground pepper to taste		

Melt the 4 tablespoons of butter in a skillet, add the mushrooms, and let them cook slowly until they are black. Season well with salt and pepper and add the 2 tablespoons of butter and the heavy cream. Let cook for a minute and spread over toasted French bread halves.

Makes about 1 cup.

Roast Corned Beef

A fine piece of brisket or rump corned beef is superb when roasted on a spit. Choose a good piece of beef with an outer coating of fat and have the butcher roll and tie it for you. Insert slivers of garlic in the meat and parboil it for 3 hours, as you would usually cook corned beef. Remove it from the liquid and let it cool. Stud the cooked corned beef with a few cloves, rub it thoroughly with prepared mustard, and arrange it on the spit. Roast it for 1 hour. Then rub the surface with a mixture of prepared mustard, dried bread crumbs, and brown sugar. Sprinkle it with a little nutmeg and plenty of coarsely ground pepper. Roast for another 30 minutes, or until the surface is nicely browned and crusty.

Lamb

Lamb should be cooked rare to medium (140° to 150°F.); it should never be well done. Whoever started well-done lamb did the animal a great deal of harm. It is very hard to get baby lamb in this country unless you live in a community where there is a Greek or an Italian butcher. Lamb is graded, as is beef, U.S. Prime, U.S. Choice, etc. For lamb, estimate approximately ¾ pound of meat per person. You may have a leg boned and tied with the shankbone left in, or spitted with the bone in. The former is much easier for the inexperienced carver.

Roast Leg of Lamb, Frénch Style

Make several gashes with a sharp knife in the leg of lamb and insert slivers of garlic. Rub the roast with salt, freshly ground pepper, and a little rosemary. Spit, balance, and roast it over a medium fire until the internal temperature reads 140° to 145°F. for rare lamb. This business of cooking it to 180°F. is destructive. Remove from the heat and let it rest or coast for 10 minutes or so before carving.

To serve: Dried beans—flageolets, white beans, or baby limas—are the traditional vegetable to serve with lamb. Soak them and boil them with an onion stuck with 2 cloves, a bay leaf, and salt to taste. When the beans are tender, drain them. Just before serving add the pan juices from the lamb and sprinkle the beans with salt and pepper. Serve a good green salad and a rosé wine to cut the richness of the lamb and beans.

Stuffed Roast Leg of Lamb, Italian Style

Have the butcher bone the roast for you but do not have him tie it. Combine 2 or 3 chopped cloves of garlic, 4 strips of bacon cut in small strips, and a handful of chopped mint leaves; salt lightly. Spread the lamb where the bone has been removed with this mixture, roll it up, and tie it securely. Spit, balance, and roast it over a medium fire until the internal temperature reads 140° to 145°F. for rare lamb.

Curry-Roasted Stuffed Leg of Lamb

Have the meat boned but not rolled. Sprinkle the interior with curry powder and salt and add pineapple slivers. Roll it up and tie it securely. Spit, balance, and roast the meat, basting with pineapple juice mixed with oil and a little additional curry powder, over a medium fire until the internal temperature reads 140° to 145°F. for rare meat.

To serve: Rice and a sauce made from the pan juices with a little more curry added and some onion and garlic make delicious accompaniments to this dish.

Roast Stuffed Shoulder of Lamb

Shoulder of lamb, boned and rolled, can be prepared in any of the ways suggested for leg of lamb. Here is another stuffing that you might like to use with the shoulder.

4	tablespoons butter	1	teaspoon fresh or dried tarragon
1	or 2 cloves garlic, chopped		Salt and freshly ground pepper to taste
2	medium onions, chopped		
¼	pound sausage meat	1	shoulder of lamb (6 pounds), boned
1½	cups bread crumbs		

Heat the butter in a skillet and add the garlic and onions. Sauté these until they are just soft. Meanwhile, cook the sausage meat in a little hot water for 5 minutes. Drain. When the garlic and onions are soft, add the cooked sausage meat, bread crumbs, and tarragon. Blend well.

Spread the inside of the shoulder with this mixture. Roll it up, tie it securely, and season to taste with salt and pepper. Spit, balance, and roast it over a medium fire until the internal temperature reads 140° to 145°F. Remove from the heat and let the meat coast or rest for 10 minutes or so before carving.

To serve: Accompany with foil-wrapped potatoes roasted in the coals or sautéed potatoes (page 175) and perhaps some corn on the cob.

Serves 6.

Roast Shoulder of Lamb Orientale

½ cup Japanese soy sauce
½ cup sherry or Madeira
3 cloves garlic, finely chopped
¼ cup finely grated gingerroot or ¼ cup minced preserved or candied ginger

1 shoulder of lamb (6 pounds), boned and rolled

Combine the soy sauce, sherry, garlic, and gingerroot and blend well. Marinate the shoulder of lamb in this mixture for 24 hours, turning frequently. Spit, balance, and roast it, basting occasionally with the marinade, until the internal temperature of the meat reaches 140° to 145°F. for rare lamb.

Serves 6.

Roast Rack of Lamb

The rack makes a delicious roast, though it is a little more delicate in flavor than most other cuts. It consists of seven or eight rib chops and, depending on the age of the lamb, will serve from two to four people. It must be boned so that the spit will go through it. Season it well with garlic, salt, and freshly ground pepper and roast it until the internal temperature reaches 140° to 145°F. for rare lamb.

To serve: Plenty of peas and new potatoes cooked

in their jackets and liberally buttered round off this course wonderfully well.

Spitted Saddle of Lamb

Saddle is the joined loin section of both sides of the backbone and includes the kidneys and flank as well as the thirteenth rib chop. Depending upon the age of the lamb, it will serve from four to six persons. A saddle of lamb is an ideal cut for a party where you wish to impress.

Insert slivers of garlic in the saddle which the butcher has tied and secured for you. (Have lamb kidneys stuffed into the saddle if you wish.) Spit the saddle parallel to the bone and roast over medium heat until the internal temperature reaches 140° to 145°F. A saddle is sliced in thin slices parallel to the backbone. The fillet and the kidneys, if they are used, should be removed at the same time.

Roast Baron of Lamb

Baron of lamb includes the saddle and two legs. In other words, it is the hind quarter. A baron of baby lamb will serve eight persons, while a young lamb makes a spectacular and exciting roast for a large number of people. Tie the legs together securely and insert slivers of garlic in the flesh. Rub the joints well with salt, freshly ground pepper, and rosemary. Balance on a spit and roast until the internal temperature reaches 140° to 145°.

This is a heller to carve, for one has to cut parallel slices from the saddle and thin slices from the legs. So study your anatomy before you attempt a baron. Know where the bones come and where the fleshiest part of the roast is.

To serve: Sautéed potatoes (page 175) and tiny new potatoes are both excellent with lamb. Also the good traditional American baked beans (page 137). Peas are a fine accompaniment and turnips are also excellent with this dish.

Roast Breast of Lamb

Spit-roasted breast of lamb makes a delicious dish. Figure on 1 pound of lamb per person. Select as lean a piece as you can find, as this cut of lamb tends to be fatty. Marinate in your favorite barbecue sauce (use one with plenty of garlic, which does things for lamb) for 2 to 3 hours. Arrange the whole breast by lacing the bones on the spit in deep scallops. Roast over a slow fire for an hour to an hour and a half, basting frequently.

Mutton

Mutton is not as well known in this country as it should be. If it is properly cooked it can be as delicious as any meat there is. For roasting on a spit, the leg and the saddle of mutton are probably the most suitable cuts. The best mutton is usually very fat, and you will want to cut away much of the excess fat or it will clog your dripping pan during the cooking procedure. Estimate approximately ¾ of a pound of mutton per person.

Like lamb, mutton is improved by seasoning with garlic. Slash small holes in the flesh and insert bits of garlic. I like the herb called "Old Man" with mutton, but not many people have bushes of it in their gardens. Spit the roast and baste it with a combination of red wine and a little oil. The wine helps to cut some of the fat. Mutton should be well salted and sprinkled with freshly ground pepper while roasting. Serve it rare. Like lamb, it is much better in flavor and texture when it is pink to red on the inside.

To serve: Perfect accompaniments to mutton are cole slaw (pages 190–191) and yellow turnips, boiled, mashed, and heavily laced with butter—a remarkable combination of flavors.

Roast Mock Venison

If this dish is properly prepared with a roast of mutton, it can give you the excellent flavor of good venison without the toughness that venison sometimes has. Use the Marinade for Game and Stew Meat (page 212) and let the mutton soak in it for two days. When you are ready to cook it, remove it from the marinade, arrange it on the spit, and roast it just to the rare stage (140° to 145°F.). Use the marinade as a baste.

Prepare a sauce by skimming all the fat from the drippings, adding any marinade that is left, 1 teaspoon of mustard, 1½ teaspoons of freshly ground pepper, and salt to taste. Bring all this to a boil and simmer gently for 5 minutes. Thicken with small balls of flour and butter kneaded together.

To serve: Accompany the mutton with the sauce, mashed turnips, potatoes, and cole slaw (pages 190–191).

Spitted Saddle of Mutton

A saddle of mutton is the two loin sections still attached to the backbone. It will serve about six persons. Have the butcher tie it securely. I have found that you can easily spit a saddle of mutton without having it boned, provided it is heavily meated. You can piqué the meat with garlic or treat it like mock venison (see previous recipe). Season it, roast it rare (140° to 145°F.), basting it frequently, and when it is done carve it the long way in thin strips. If you cut the saddle along the bone —parallel to the spinal bone—you will get the meat in thin, fine strips. Don't forget the delicious, tender fillet on the inside of the saddle.

Pork

Pork can be as delicious a meat as one can prepare on the outdoor grill if it is slow-roasted and well basted. Allow ¾ of a pound per person with the bone in (particularly with the loin). One pound of boneless meat will serve two to three persons. The loin, the shoulder, and the fresh ham all lend themselves to outdoor cooking. The fresh ham and shoulder should be boned, rolled, and tied before balancing on the spit. If it is possible, the skin should be left on. Many Italian shops will stuff a boned and rolled fresh ham or shoulder with fresh basil, garlic, parsley, and other savory bits, which makes for perfect spit roasting.

It is well to remember that pork must be cooked through. There must be an internal temperature of about 175° to 180°F. to ensure doneness without losing the desirable natural juices.

Roast Loin of Pork

Buy a whole loin of pork and have it boned. Sprinkle the two halves with thyme, salt, and freshly ground pepper, and add some onion slices. Tie it together securely, spit it, and roast until the internal temperature reaches 175°F. Meanwhile, baste the pork with drippings and a little beer. When done it should have a nice glaze on the outside.

To serve: If you prepare some parsnips and sweet potatoes by boiling them in salted water until they are just short of done, and then add them to the dripping pan for the last half hour, you will find them a tasty addition to your roast pork. Mix freshly grated horseradish and applesauce as a zippy accompaniment to cut the richness of the meat.

Roast Stuffed Loin of Pork

Put prunes to soak in sherry or white wine and pit them or not, as you choose. Cut down through the flesh of each half of boned loin and stuff it with the prunes. Sprinkle the stuffing with a little nutmeg, press the halves together, and tie securely. Rub the outside of the meat with salt, freshly ground pepper, and a little thyme. Spit it and roast until the pork is thoroughly done. When you carve the meat, you slice right down through stuffing and all.

To serve: I like this dish accompanied with sautéed

potatoes (page 175) and new cabbage, either steamed or sautéed in bacon fat until just wilted, and seasoned with salt, freshly ground pepper, and a dash of vinegar.

Roast Fresh Ham

If you have the time and the patience, roasting a whole fresh ham on the spit will give you a truly succulent feast for a large party. A whole bone-in fresh ham will weigh around 13 pounds and will serve about 16 to 20 people. The fire must not be too hot, for the meat must cook slowly.

Have your butcher leave the skin on the ham and bone and tie it for you. Score the skin in diamond shapes or in strips so that it will form crisp bits of cracklings as the ham cooks. Salt and pepper the meat well and rub a little thyme or thyme seasoning powder into the surface. Sprinkle it with ground ginger, or fresh grated gingerroot if it is available.

Arrange the ham on the spit and roast very slowly, brushing the meat with the Basting Sauce for Fresh Ham (page 95). The meat will take about 25 minutes or more per pound to cook. It should reach an internal temperature of 185°F. on a meat thermometer.

To serve: Carve the ham in thin slices and put some of the crackling skin on each piece of meat. With this serve thin slices of tart apple that have been sautéed in butter with a little sugar added, and slices of large onions steamed in butter. Simply slice large onions into thick pieces, put them in a skillet with about 5 tablespoons of butter, cover, and cook slowly until tender. Do not let them brown—rather let them steam in their own juice and the melted butter. Just before serving, add ½ cup of grated cheese, preferably imported Swiss, to the onions.

Basting Sauce for Fresh Ham

1 cup orange juice
½ cup lemon juice
1 cup oil or melted pork fat
1 teaspoon thyme

1 tablespoon grated gingerroot or 1 teaspoon ground ginger
3 tablespoons soy sauce

Combine all ingredients and blend well.

Makes 2½ cups sauce.

Roast Suckling Pig

Suckling pigs range in size from around 9 to 18 or 20 pounds and it takes a rather large spit to roast one. Allow 1 pound of meat per person and if you have ample equipment, here is an excellent way to do it. Full grown pigs need an improvised spit and must be turned by hand.

Choose a pig weighing about 12 pounds and clean it thoroughly. Sprinkle the inside with salt, freshly ground pepper, and a little oregano or sweet basil. Rub the skin well with oil and salt and a little of the same herb. Arrange the pig on the spit so that it is perfectly balanced and roast for 2 to 2½ hours, basting often with the pan drippings. Some people like to prepare the skin with a mixture of honey, lemon juice, and oregano.

To serve: Accompany it with sauerkraut which you have steamed in beer and seasoned with garlic and coarse black pepper. Pass around a heaping dish of ice-cold applesauce. Beer is an excellent drink with this dish.

Here's how to carve the pig: Cut along the spinal column, cutting the pig in half. Remove each ham. Slice the hams and cut through the ribs. Serve each person a little of the rib meat and a little of the ham.

Traditionally, suckling pig is decorated before it is brought to the table. A necklace of raw cranberries, two cranberries for the eyes, and an apple in the mouth is the usual thing. I'm just as happy with suckling pig served without any costume at all.

Serves 12 to 14.

Stuffed Suckling Pig

1	suckling pig (12 pounds), liver reserved		Salt and freshly ground pepper to taste
	Oil	5	to 6 cups dry bread crumbs
	Salt		
5	tablespoons pork fat or butter	¼	cup chopped parsley
2	medium onions, very finely chopped	1	tablespoon basil or rosemary
2	cloves garlic, very finely chopped	½	cup shelled pistachio or pine nuts
	Liver (reserved from pig), finely chopped	½	cup sherry or cognac
		2	tablespoons butter

Clean the pig thoroughly and rub the skin with oil and salt. Melt the pork fat in a skillet and add the onions and garlic. When they are just soft but not colored, add the liver and sauté for a minute or two. Season with salt and pepper to taste and tranfer to a large bowl. Add the remaining ingredients and mix well. Stuff the pig and sew it up securely. Spit and roast it as Roast Suckling Pig (pages 95–96) until beautifully browned and crisp.

To serve: Make a sauce with the pan drippings, ¼ pound of finely chopped mushrooms, ½ cup of chopped parsley, and 1 teaspoon of dry mustard. Season with salt and freshly ground pepper to taste.

Also accompany this suckling pig with iced applesauce and steamed Brussels sprouts. Simply put the Brussels sprouts in a skillet with a little water (not more than ½ cup) and 3 tablespoons of butter. Salt and pepper to taste, cover, and simmer until just barely done. They should still be crisp. Remove the cover and cook them down for a minute or two over a high flame. Be careful not to let them burn. Add more butter and serve.

Serves 12 to 14.

Barbecued Pig

I shall never forget the first barbecued pig I ate in the West Indies. It was a good many years ago but it still remains one of the gastronomical highlights of my life. I wish I could duplicate it often, but it takes ample space and plenty of help.

On this occasion, the pig weighed about 50 pounds. One of the household servants started a wood fire early in the dawn and let it cook down to glowing coals. The fire was built right on the ground and forked poles were arranged over it to hold the pig. A large number of stones were put to heat in the fire and as the fire burned down more and more wood was added to build a great bank of coals.

A basting sauce was made for the barbecue of 2 cups of oil, 1 cup of white wine, 1 cup of sour orange juice (we don't get the sour oranges in this country, but a substitute may be made by adding about 1 part lemon juice to 2 parts orange), 1 tablespoon of oregano, some freshly grated gingerroot, 1 tablespoon of salt, 1 tablespoon of freshly ground pepper, and a little of the wild herb called cilantro in the South, Chinese parsley in New York and San Francisco, and coriander other places.

When the coals were glowing hot, the inside of the pig was stuffed with some of the hot stones from the fire, the pig was spitted on a large stick and hung over the coals to roast. It cooked for hours, being turned by hand every so often and basted constantly with the sauce. The basting tool was a bunch of corn husks tied onto the end of a stick. For the last hour of cooking, plantains were arranged in the coals under the pig, so that the pork juices would drop down and permeate them while they roasted. When the pig was done, the skin was crisp and pungent with the spices of the sauce, the meat was tender, juicy, and thoroughly done. Nothing ever tasted so good.

Spitted Spareribs

Soak spareribs in soy sauce for an hour. Rub them with chopped garlic or a little thyme or oregano. Arrange the whole sides of spareribs by lacing them on the spit in deep scallops. Figure on a pound of spareribs per person. They should be roasted over a slow fire for an hour to an hour and a half and basted occasionally with the marinade. This makes them succulent and brings out the flavor.

To serve: Accompany the spareribs with white bean or lentil salad (pages 192–193) and a sauce for the ribs made as follows: Put about ½ jar of apricot jam in a saucepan with a little lemon juice and let it cook down for 10 minutes. Mix 3 tablespoons of dry mustard with 4 tablespoons of white wine or sherry and add this to the jam.

Roast Chinese Spareribs

1 clove garlic	Drop of red food coloring
1 small can Chinese bean sauce	
1 small can hoisin sauce	1 cup cooking oil
1 teaspoon salt	1 cup sugar
	1 pound spareribs per person

Combine the garlic, bean sauce, hoisin sauce, salt, and coloring in the jar of a blender. Blend for 2 minutes. (If you do not have a blender, mince the garlic and bean sauce together and blend well with the hoisin sauce, salt, and coloring.) Add the oil and sugar and mix well.

Marinate spareribs overnight or for several hours, turning them often in this mixture. Weave on the spit and roast over a medium fire for an hour and a half, basting or brushing them with the marinade from time to time during the cooking process.

Roast Polynesian Spareribs

4 teaspoons dry mustard	1 teaspoon fennel
½ cup sherry	1 teaspoon aniseed
¼ cup soy sauce	1 teaspoon cinnamon
2 cups apricot jam	1 pound spareribs per
1 teaspoon cloves	person

Combine the mustard, sherry, soy sauce, and apricot jam and blend well. Add the cloves, fennel, aniseed, and cinnamon. Coat the spareribs well with this mixture and let them stand for an hour. Weave them on the spit and roast over a slow fire for an hour to an hour and a half, brushing them occasionally with the marinade.

To serve: Foil-wrapped potatoes cooked in the ashes, grilled tomatoes (page 180), and sauerkraut go exceptionally well with spareribs.

Makes 2¾ cups marinade.

NOTE: Bean sauce and hoisin sauce may be purchased in Oriental food stores.

SPIT-ROASTED POULTRY

Spit-roasted chicken, turkey, and duck have a flavor that no oven roasting can ever give them, plus a superb crispy skin. People have a tendency to overcook chickens, and this is true of spit roasting as well as oven roasting. A chicken is done when the leg and thigh joint move back and forth freely. This is really the only test you can make. With a large bird, the meat thermometer is inserted in the thick part of the thigh without touching the bone. It will register about 180°F. when the turkey or large chicken is ready.

The following general instructions may be followed for poultry and game on any spit-roasting unit; variations will be noted in the recipes for specific dishes:

- Select young, plump, tender poultry.
- Wash if necessary, remove hair and pinfeathers by singeing; dry well (inside and out) with a soft cloth.
- Season inside (not outside) according to taste; stuff if desired; close opening with poultry pins or skewers, or sew with strong thread.
- Truss and tie securely. Tie string around legs, then cross over breast around wings and back to legs, or fasten wings to body and tie ends of legs together.
- If you insert the spit just in back of the tail of the bird and bring it out in the side of the breastbone, you will get a good balance for your bird. If you are doing two or more birds on the spit, alternate them with the breast of one against the leg of the next. One should be back on top, the next stomach on top, and so on.

Chicken

Young plump birds that are usually broiled make excellent eating if seasoned and roasted on a spit. If you buy the small broilers, figure one chicken to each serving. A good-sized broiler (2 to 2½ pounds) will serve two persons very nicely.

Tarragon-Roasted Chicken

Butter the chickens well and rub them with a little tarragon seasoning powder—or use fresh tarragon if it is available. Sprinkle some of the herb inside the chickens, too. Truss the birds firmly so that they will hold their shape. Several small birds or two larger birds will fit on one spit. Be sure to arrange them on the spit so that they are properly balanced to ensure evenness of cooking.

Roast chickens from 30 minutes to 1 hour, depending on their size. I don't like chicken overdone—it loses some of its juiciness and flavor. For me, the meat at the joint of a perfectly done chicken still has a slightly pinkish cast.

I like to baste chicken with a mixture of equal parts of melted butter and white wine, with salt and sometimes a little paprika added. This gives the birds a nice glaze and leaves delicious pan juices.

To serve: Plain watercress—no dressing on it—and crisp fried potatoes go well with these small chickens. To me, the usual gravy-and-mashed-potatoes is out of key with this delicate morsel.

Rosemary-Roasted Chicken

Substitute rosemary for the tarragon in the seasoning for Tarragon-Roasted Chicken (page 100) and roast in the same way.

Onion-Stuffed Roast Chicken

Stuff the chicken with a few tiny white onions which have been peeled and browned in butter for about 10 minutes. Sew the chicken up before you truss it.

To serve: Accompany the chicken with more tiny white onions cooked in butter until brown and just soft.

Stuffed Chicken

Here is an excellent way to make an extra-fancy dish of spitted broilers.

2 broilers (2 to 2½ pounds each), left whole, livers reserved	½ cup cognac or whiskey
4 tablespoons butter	1 cup dry bread crumbs
1 small onion, chopped	Generous dash of tarragon or tarragon seasoning powder
1 pound veal, finely ground	Salt to taste
¼ pound chicken livers (plus reserved livers), ground or finely chopped	2 eggs White wine Melted butter

Wipe the insides of the chickens with a damp cloth.

Heat the butter in a large skillet and sauté the onion until soft. Add the veal and toss it around in the pan to separate it. Add the chicken livers and cognac and let the mixture simmer for 5 minutes. Remove from heat and add the bread crumbs, tarragon, salt, and eggs. Mix well.

Stuff the chickens with the mixture and sew them up. Truss them, spit them, and cook as Tarragon-Roasted Chicken (page 100), basting with a half-and-half mixture of white wine and melted butter. These stuffed chickens will take a little longer to cook than unstuffed chickens.

To serve: Split each chicken in half, serve a half heaped with stuffing on each plate. Pour the pan juices over each serving. A good green salad is enough with this dish, which is rich and filling and doesn't need the addition of potatoes.

Serves 4.

Roast Chicken with Cream Sauce

The French have a very interesting method of preparing chicken under a roasting unit. For this dish use a chicken big enough to serve four people, or two of the larger broilers. Roast plain, basting with just a little melted butter and salt. When the chicken is cooked, remove it from the heating unit, pour over it ½ cup of cognac, and ignite to blaze. Put on a hot platter to carve.

Collect the drippings, add 1 cup of heavy cream and 3 egg yolks. Heat slowly over a low flame, stirring constantly. Be careful the sauce does not boil or it will curdle. When it is hot and nicely thickened, taste for seasoning and add a little cognac.

To serve: Accompany the chicken with the sauce and add rice and greens to make a delicious meal.

Serves 4.

Garlic-Roasted Chicken

1	roasting chicken (4 to 5 pounds)	2	tablespoons butter
4	cloves garlic		Juice of 1 lemon
¼	pound butter		Salt and freshly ground pepper to taste
	Large sprig of parsley		

Wipe the inside of the chicken with a damp cloth. Mash 2 of the cloves of garlic and blend with the ¼ pound of butter. Let this garlic butter stand 30 minutes. Meanwhile, finely chop the remaining 2 cloves of garlic and sprinkle them inside the cavity of the chicken. Add the parsley and the 2 tablespoons of butter and close the vent with foil. Truss the chicken well.

Melt the garlic butter and add the lemon juice and salt and pepper. Roast the chicken on a spit, basting it frequently with the melted butter mixture.

Serves 4.

Baby Chickens on the Spit

These little delicacies are called *poussin*, squab chickens, or baby pullets, and weigh ¾ to 1 pound each. Plan at least one to a person, more for those with hearty appetites. Spit, brush with plenty of seasoned butter, and roast them quickly, being careful not to overcook. Brush frequently during the cooking with melted butter.

To serve: If you are fortunate enough to have your own garden, dig a few hills of very small new potatoes. Cook them in their jackets and drench them with melted butter, salt, and freshly ground pepper. Add, if you wish, some chopped parsley or a few finely chopped chives. Tiny French peas are also an exquisite addition to this menu.

Capon

A capon is a fat, tender bird—a choice dish for the table. It needs no embellishments and is best when served plain in all its delicious glory. A large capon weighs up to 8 or 9 pounds, and will not fit into many of the smaller grilling units. Following the trend in turkeys, capon raisers have been developing smaller birds (4 to 5 pounds) which are just as fat and tender as the traditional big ones. Look for one that fits your cooking space. Simply truss it, spit it, and roast it plain, basting with a little butter. Salt and pepper toward the end of the cooking process.

To serve: Crisp fried potatoes and watercress go well with this succulent bird.

Turkey

Small turkeys spitted and roasted are superb, but even a large 18- to 20-pound turkey can be cooked to perfection in this manner if you have the equipment to handle it. A turkey should be basted frequently, and my choice is equal parts of melted butter and white wine or dry vermouth. Test doneness by moving the legs back and forth to see if they are loose. If you use a meat thermometer, remove the turkey at 170° to 175°F. In buying turkey, plan at least 1 pound per person. Allow 18 to 20 minutes a pound roasting time.

Stuffed Turkey

This will take a little longer to cook than unstuffed turkey and must be perfectly balanced on your spit, so tie it securely. The stuffing will take the place of a starch dish and cut down on the preparations for the dinner. Allow 1 cup of stuffing for each pound of turkey. A 12-pound bird uses 8 cups of cooked rice.

1	turkey (12 pounds)	1	cup chopped pistachio
6	tablespoons butter		nuts
1	cup finely chopped	1	teaspoon rosemary
	green onions		Salt and freshly
1	cup finely chopped		ground pepper to
	parsley		taste
8	cups cooked rice	¼	pound butter, melted
1	cup finely chopped	1	cup Madeira or
	chicken livers or		½ cup cognac
	turkey livers		Seasoned butter
1	cup finely chopped ham		

Wipe the cavity of the turkey with a damp cloth. Heat the 6 tablespoons butter in a large skillet and simmer the green onions and parsley for about 5 minutes. Add the remaining ingredients, except the seasoned butter, and mix gently.

Stuff the turkey lightly and sew up the vent or close it with small skewers. Remove the neck and secure the skin at the neck cavity in the same manner. Truss the bird, rub it with seasoned butter, spit it, and roast it over medium coals for about 4½ hours, or until it reaches an internal temperature of 175°F. Baste it with equal parts of melted butter and white wine, dry vermouth, Madeira, or cognac.

To serve: If you want to take the trouble to make a giblet gravy in the kitchen and bring it out, it is quite good served on the stuffing. Also, if you feel in the mood, a huge bowl of mashed potatoes would grace this meal.

Serves 12.

Roast Turkey Flambé
This dish has an exceptionally delicious sauce and makes fine party fare; guests are apt to ask you for the recipe.

1	turkey (8 pounds)	4	tablespoons butter
	Melted butter	1½	cups dairy sour cream
	White wine		Dash of cognac
¼	cup cognac		
	Cooked turkey giblets, broth reserved		

Truss, skewer, and roast the turkey over a medium fire for about 1¼ to 1¾ hours, basting well with a mixture of equal parts of melted butter and white wine. When it is done (internal temperature 170° to 175°F.) remove it to a hot ovenproof platter or a board. Heat the ¼ cup cognac slightly, pour it over the turkey, and ignite. When the flames die down, pour off the juices into a cup. Keep the turkey warm.

Chop the giblets and sauté briefly in the 4 tablespoons of butter. (Do this in a pan on the grill, in an electric skillet, or in a chafing dish.) To the giblets add the reserved juices and a little of the reserved giblet broth. Taste for seasoning, blend well, and heat thoroughly. Stir in the sour cream, blend, and heat, but do not allow to boil or it will curdle. Add the dash of cognac and serve with the turkey.

Serves 8.

Rolled Roast Turkey

This is a popular method for spitting or roasting turkeys nowadays. Have your butcher do it or try this process yourself. (Rolled and tied turkeys are available in some supermarkets and poultry shops, ready for the oven.) If you do it yourself, skin the turkey, trying to keep the skin intact, then bone the turkey, keeping it as whole as possible. If you start from the side of the backbone and work with a sharp knife along the bones, you will not find this a difficult job. Lay the boned turkey meat on the skin. Season with salt, freshly ground pepper, and tarragon and spread well with softened butter. Roll tightly and tie firmly with butcher's twine. Rub with butter or oil and spit and balance it.

Cook until the meat thermometer registers about 165°F., approximately 22 to 30 minutes per pound of ready-to-roast weight (small roasts take the longer time). Let it rest for about 15 minutes before removing from the spit. Turkey prepared this way is perfect for carving.

Duck

Roast Duck

To prepare Long Island duckling and other domestic varieties, spit the duckling and roast until nearly done. Baste during the last few minutes with a mixture of 2 tablespoons of soy sauce, 4 tablespoons of sherry, white wine, or whiskey, 2 tablespoons of honey, and a few slivers of gingerroot. This will give the crisp skin a nice flavor and a high glaze. The duck will take about 1½ hours to cook.

To serve: Cut in quarters with poultry shears or a heavy knife.

Variation

You may vary the basting sauce by adding curry powder to taste, garlic to taste, a little orange juice and grated orange rind, or use any of the sauces given under the recipes for broiled duckling.

Goose

Goose, unfortunately an almost forgotten delicacy, is a national delight. Roasting on a spit is an excellent method for cooking geese, since it retains the moisture but eliminates much of the fat. An 8-pound goose will serve 4 to 6.

Roast Goose

Select a good fat 8- to 10-pound goose. Cut away the excess fat from the inside. Render it and save. Rub the interior with half a lemon and then with thyme seasoning powder and salt. Add a couple of onions and sew up the goose. Balance it, arrange it on the spit, and be sure it is well placed. Roast it over medium coals without basting. Prick the skin in several places to let the fat escape. Watch the dripping pan. The fat will collect there at a great rate and it must be emptied. Test the goose for doneness by puncturing the thigh with a sharp fork. When the juice no longer runs pinkish the bird is done. It should take about 2 to 2½ hours to cook, and when done the skin should be very crisp and brown.

To serve: Goose with puréed chestnuts heated with butter, and sauerkraut cooked for several hours with white wine makes a wonderful dinner. The tang of the kraut is just what is needed to cut the richness of goose.

Serves 6 to 8.

Garlic-Stuffed Roast Goose

Season the inside of an 8- to 10-pound goose with salt and freshly ground pepper. Stuff it with as many peeled and crushed cloves of garlic as it will hold (about 2 pounds). Truss, spit, and roast the goose over medium coals for about 2 to 2½ hours. Remove garlic before eating.

Serves 6 to 8.

GAME

Venison

There are so many grades of venison shot by hunters that it is difficult to know how tender or how tough the meat will be. For this reason, as well as to enhance the gamey flavor, it is a good idea to marinate venison for several days before roasting it. Use the Marinade for Game and Stew Meat (page 212). I usually let venison stand for two days or longer in a marinade.

Roast Saddle of Venison

The saddle (whole loin section) is by far the most delicious part of the animal. Allow ¾ to 1 pound of meat for each person. After it has been marinated (see above), arrange it on the spit and roast it over a medium fire, basting often with the marinade, until it is crispy on the outside but still rare in the middle. It should take about an hour to an hour and a half, depending on the size of the animal. Carve as you would a saddle of mutton or lamb—parallel to the bone.

To serve: Accompany the saddle with chestnuts, either whole or puréed (both are available unsweetened in cans), and a sauce made from the marinade seasoned with freshly ground pepper, dry mustard, and a little A-1 sauce. Blend these together and cook down for a few minutes. For my taste, you can omit the currant jelly and serve a good bottle of red wine instead.

Roast Haunch of Venison

Allow ¾ to 1 pound of meat for each person and have your butcher bone and tie the haunch for you so that it will fit on the spit. Soak it in the Marinade for Game and Stew Meat (page 212) for several days and roast it over a medium fire for an hour to an hour and a half, just to the rare stage, basting often with the marinade. Add a little oil to the marinade for lubrication.

To serve: Make a sauce with the marinade and drippings flavored with a little onion and thicken with small balls of kneaded butter and flour.

Pheasant

Pheasant, one of the most delicious and highly prized game birds, has a tendency to be dry unless it is thoroughly lubricated during the cooking process. It should never be cooked for too long, for an overcooked pheasant is bound to be dry and tasteless. Fast cooking over high heat will give you juicy rare meat. One pheasant will serve two people.

I consider it useless to stuff a pheasant. In the first place, since these birds should be cooked so quickly, the stuffing never has a chance to mellow. In the second place, pheasant has a delightful flavor of its own that needs no dressing up.

Roast Pheasant

Rub the inside of the birds with a little salt and freshly ground pepper and perhaps a little herb—thyme or rosemary—or a few juniper berries. Cover the breast with a thin slice of salt pork or bacon rind to keep it lubricated. Truss and arrange on the spit. Roast it very quickly, testing the leg joints to see if they are movable and tender. Do not overcook.

To serve: The plain pan juices, some potato chips (page 175), and crisp greens are good accompaniments with this bird. I think pheasant needs a good bottle of wine and some substantial sweet course after it.

Roast Pheasant with Cream Sauce

Prepare and roast the pheasant as above until tender. Remove the spit and take the piece of salt pork from the breast. Pour ½ cup of cognac or whiskey over the bird and ignite. Remove most of the fat from the dripping pan and add 1 cup of heavy cream to the pan. Heat without letting it boil. Add small balls of butter and flour kneaded together and stir until slightly thickened. Season to taste with salt and freshly ground pepper.

To serve: Crisp fried potatoes and a green salad are perfect accompaniments. Red wine is an absolute must.

Roast Pheasant with Sauerkraut

If the pheasant is an old one and apt to be tough and stringy, roast it plain according to directions for Roast Pheasant (page 110). When it is done, cut it in quarters and add it to 3 pounds of sauerkraut which has been cooked in white wine for 3 hours. Add a slice or two of garlic sausage, a few whole peppercorns, and some more white wine—about 2 cups. Grate a clove of garlic over all, cover tightly, and steam for 2 hours. This is an unusual and tasty dish and a sure way to have tender pheasant.

To serve: A delicate white wine goes nicely with this dish.

Partridge

This is my favorite game bird, and I like it done simply as its flavor needs no enhancing. While the French partridge can't be beaten, the American variety is still excellent. Allow one bird per person, more if you have invited hearty eaters.

Roast Partridge

Salt and pepper the birds and perhaps put a few juniper berries inside them. Cover the breasts well with salt pork, arrange the birds diagonally on the spit, and roast them quickly. They should take about 20 to 30 minutes to cook, and though they should not be overcooked, neither are they good eaten very rare. About medium is right for them. Test at the thigh to see how done they are.

To serve: It is traditional to serve partridge on toast spread with pâté of partridge giblets (page 67). This is truly superb eating.

Squab

Squab are hardly the most practical dish for outdoor eating, but if well lubricated with salt pork and roasted to a turn on a spit, they are exceedingly good. Squab weigh from ¾ of a pound to 1½ pounds. Certainly for hearty outdoor appetites you will want to figure on at least one bird per serving, maybe two or three if they are very small.

Roast Squab

Season the squab with a little salt and freshly ground pepper and a sprinkling of thyme or rosemary, if you like. Nothing else. Wrap their breasts well with salt pork. Spit them and roast from 30 minutes to 1 hour, depending on their size. Unlike other poultry, squab should be well done, but be careful not to let it get dry and tasteless.

To serve: Potato chips (page 175) or crisp French fried potatoes (page 174), green peas, and green olives seem to go well with this bird.

Quail

There are two different types of quail in this country —both very small. I've seen one person eat as many as six quail with great zest all the way, but one or two per person is a more usual serving. As with other game, quail should be cooked carefully so that they do not dry out during cooking.

Roast Quail

Wrap the breasts of the birds well with salt pork or bacon and arrange them sideways on the spit. If you wish, you may put a dash of thyme or tarragon or a few juniper berries in the interior of each quail. Roast quickly, basting with melted butter, for these small morsels need every bit of fat possible. They will take about 15 to 20 minutes to cook—depending on their size. Season to taste.

To serve: Avoid serving anything with quail that competes with their delicate flavor. Cornbread or potatoes and plenty of greens go extremely well with them.

Wild Duck

Unlike Long Island or Pekin duck, the wild varieties do not have the heavy layer of fat next to the skin, and so are much less greasy eating. They are at their best if they have been hung and are served very rare. Allow one bird per person.

Roast Wild Duck

Rub the duck with a half lemon, inside and out. I like to put an onion stuck with 2 cloves in the interior of each duck. Butter well on the skin and arrange on the spit. Roast rapidly for about 15 to 18 minutes, basting with melted butter and red wine. The flesh should be red and rare when cut, to my way of thinking, but test at the thigh and judge for yourself. Season to taste.

To serve: Apples, green peas, and turnips are customarily served with wild duck. Another traditional accompaniment—wild rice combined with finely chopped toasted almonds—tastes wonderful but seems to me a little pretentious for outdoor eating. Don't waste the wonderful pan juices—serve them with the duck.

Roast Wild Duck with Wine Sauce

Prepare and roast the ducks as on page 113. When they are done, remove them from the heating unit and pour about ½ cup of cognac or whiskey over them and blaze. Carve the ducks. Combine the juices from the carving, the pan juices, and ½ cup of red wine. Season to taste and heat. Serve as is, or thicken with small balls of kneaded butter and flour.

FISH

Spitted Fish

Large fish such as salmon, haddock, cod, tuna, sturgeon, and some members of the bass family may be spitted and roasted over charcoal. Allow about 1 pound undressed weight for each person. The fish must be tied securely or wired to the spit. Some people make a wire basket, which they line with ferns, that will fit on the spit. Baste the fish with olive oil and lemon juice blended together.

Foil-Roasted Stuffed Fish

Whole large fish may be rolled in aluminum foil which has been buttered or oiled and either roasted directly in the coals or roasted on the grill. The advantage of using foil is that you may stuff the fish with any savory stuffing you desire, or with thinly sliced raw onions, peppers, tomatoes, and sprigs of parsley, well lubricated with butter or oil. You will be assured that the juices will not run out and that you will have a perfectly flavored fish when it is finished.

NOTE: Small fish may be cooked in the same manner, although I recommend a double coating of foil for them.

SKEWER & SKILLET COOKING

SKEWER COOKING

Broiling in skewers is one of the oldest known forms of cookery. The early nomadic peoples of Asia and the Near East strung pieces of meat and vegetables on sticks and cooked them over the fire. This was the forerunner of the popular skewer cookery of today. For centuries the Japanese have cooked on skewers over the *hibachi*—a cast-iron tub with a grill over its top, set in a small decorative table or on a stand that can be used on a table. The charcoal is ignited outdoors in the *hibachi*, which is brought indoors after the charcoal has stopped smoking and turned to glowing coals.

The French have cooked on skewers for generations. They call it *en brochette*, and many of the choice items on the menus in French restaurants are cooked this way. This type of cookery can be done in front of or above your charcoal fire, or in any broiler or electric grill. Some grills have wheels with several skewers attached for cooking dishes *en brochette*. If you buy your own skewers you have a wide choice, from the simplest functional types to fancy designs copied from decorative old French *brochettes*.

Many foods cooked on skewers should be marinated for from several hours up to a day or so before grilling. Others, such as the *hibachi* recipes, are marinated for only 30 minutes to 2 hours.

Vegetables

Fresh vegetables may be combined and strung on skewers, brushed with oil or butter, and broiled over charcoal. Almost any combination you like may be cooked this way. For example, eggplant sections, tomato wedges, and mushrooms. The same combination may be used with onion sections. Parboiled onions, tomatoes, partly cooked or canned potatoes, green pepper slices are all excellent for skewer cookery—in fact, the combinations of vegetables that can be used are practically endless.

Beef

Skewered Tenderloin

Buy tenderloin or fillet in one piece. Cut in cubes 1½ x 2 inches. Arrange these on skewers, alternating with mushroom caps and chunks of onion, if you wish. Season with salt and freshly ground pepper and brush with melted beef fat. (Get some suet at the butcher's and melt it if you don't have any in your refrigerator.) Grill quickly over charcoal or in your electric unit until the meat is nicely browned but rare and juicy inside. This should take from 4 to 6 minutes.

To serve: Fry potatoes in beef fat and accompany with a large bowl of greens and French bread.

Sirloin, Moyen Age

Cut your sirloin steak into cubes 1½ x 2 inches. Dust

well with rosemary seasoning powder or roll in dried rosemary. Season with salt and alternate the chunks on skewers with small ripe tomatoes or tomato wedges. Grill quickly over charcoal or in the electric unit. Turn several times to cook evenly.

To serve: A salad of cold string beans and finely chopped onion with a good French dressing and fried potatoes or baked stuffed potatoes go well with this dish.

Tenderized Beef Cubes

Buy a chunk of one of the tougher cuts of beef—chuck or round. Cut it into cubes and sprinkle each cube with meat tenderizer (I prefer it nonseasoned). Use 1 teaspoon per pound and let the meat stand at room temperature for 1 hour. Arrange on skewers, alternating with mushroom caps or chunks of onion. Brush with melted beef fat and season with salt and freshly ground pepper. Broil over charcoal or in your electric unit until nicely browned on all sides but still rare in the middle.

To serve: Crisp French fried onions (page 179) and French bread are delicious with this beef.

Stuffed Beef Rolls

Cut thin strips of sirloin or tenderloin, about 4 inches long and 1 inch wide. Roll each strip around—alternately—a stuffed olive, an oyster (lightly puffed in hot water), a small parboiled onion, or a mushroom cap. Fasten each with a toothpick, brush with melted butter, and arrange four to a skewer. Broil quickly and season with salt and freshly ground pepper.

Marinated Peppered-Beef Cubes

Marinate cubes of beef in olive oil and chopped onion. Roll them in coarsely ground or cracked black pepper. Alternate the cubes on skewers with small tomatoes or mushrooms. Broil until nicely browned on all sides but rare in the center.

Soy Beef Strips

Marinate thin strips of beef tenderloin in soy sauce seasoned with grated garlic. Sprinkle with black pepper, loop onto skewers, and broil quickly.

Piquant Beef Cubes

Make a paste with horseradish, grated onion, a little dry mustard, and red wine. Marinate cubes of tender beef in this for about 2 hours. Arrange on skewers, season with salt and freshly ground pepper, and broil until browned on the outside but still rare in the center. Brush with the paste once during the broiling.

Skewered Beefsteak and Vegetables

Skewer cubes of beefsteak with tiny onions, tiny tomatoes, and small canned potatoes. Add small hunks of beef fat here and there on the skewer. Brush with melted butter, and broil quickly. Season to taste.

Lamb

Shish Kebab

Buy a leg or a shoulder of lamb. Although the leg is more expensive, it will give you more meat for your money. Figure about ½ to ¾ of a pound of meat per serving. This is lip-smacking food and people like generous amounts of it.

Cut the lamb into 2-inch-square cubes and marinate (pages 210–211) for a few hours or up to 48 hours. The longer they stand, the tastier they are. When you are ready to broil, arrange the cubes on skewers. You may use just meat or meat alternated with any of the following: Onion chunks, tomato wedges or small whole tomatoes, mushroom caps, pineapple cubes or wedges, eggplant cubes, zucchini slices, whole pickled onions.

Broil over charcoal or in the electric grill, turning often until nicely browned and crispy on the outside but still pink and juicy in the middle.

To serve: Rice or *kasha* (steamed buckwheat, sold in grocery stores as groats) is traditional; buttered toasted finger rolls, or French, Italian, or Armenian bread heated slightly.

Shashlik I

This recipe for the Russian form of shish kebab is from my favorite Russian restaurant in Paris, and it seems to me a delicious version.

Cut lamb in cubes as for shish kebab and marinate up to 36 hours in olive oil to cover, seasoned with 4 finely chopped onions, 1 teaspoon of salt, and 1 or more teaspoons of thyme. Arrange the shashlik on skewers and grill over charcoal or in the electric grill until nicely crisp on the outside but still pink and juicy in the middle.

To serve: Remove the lamb from the skewers and accompany with rice, small tomatoes, and green onions.

Shashlik II

This shashlik has a slightly different marinade and different accompaniments.

Marinate the lamb cubes in olive oil, salt, freshly ground pepper, garlic, and thyme up to 36 hours. Arrange the lamb cubes on skewers and broil over charcoal or in the electric grill until brown and nicely crisp on the outside but still pink inside.

To serve: Remove the meat from the skewers and accompany with *kasha* (steamed buckwheat), dairy sour cream, and capers.

Lamb Javanese

Cut paper-thin slices of leg or shoulder of lamb, and then cut the slices into 1-inch squares. String them on small skewers and marinate in Javanese Marinade (page 211) for 2 hours. Broil quickly over charcoal or in a broiler until the meat is just heated through and glazed.

To serve: Sliced and buttered French, Italian, or Armenian bread goes well with this dish, which makes a pleasant appetizer served with drinks.

Variety Meats

Liver and lamb kidneys lend themselves to skewer cookery. You will find recipes for grilled veal kidneys on pages 55–56.

Skewered Liver

Wrap small pieces of chicken, calf's, or lamb liver in pieces of partially cooked bacon, run them on skewers, and broil until the bacon is crisp.

Skewered Lamb Kidneys

Plan on three lamb kidneys to a person when you order from the butcher. Soak the kidneys in milk or salt water for 1 hour, then remove the core of gristle from each. Put 3 kidneys, covered with partially cooked bacon strips, on each skewer. Add mushroom caps at each end of the skewer, and grill. Brush with melted butter, oil, or English mustard during the grilling. Season with salt and freshly ground pepper just before serving.

Chicken

Other recipes for skewer-broiled chicken are with Japanese Dishes (pages 125–129).

Chicken Javanese

Remove the bones from 2 or 3 large chicken breasts and pound them with a mallet until they are flattened. Spread them with butter and roll them. Cut the rolled breasts into thin slices and string them on small skewers. Marinate in Javanese Marinade (page 211) for 2 hours. Broil over charcoal or in the electric rotisserie for about 3 minutes.

To serve: Accompany the chicken slices with chutney and toasted almonds or filberts. This is a delicious appetizer.

Fish

Fish fillets can be laced onto skewers, looped back and forth, and broiled in any of the following ways:

● Brush with melted butter, season with salt and freshly ground pepper, and broil until just a pale golden brown. Add a dash of lemon juice.

● Dip the fillets in melted butter and roll them in bread crumbs before looping them on skewers. Broil, and just before they are done, season them with salt and freshly ground pepper and dust them heavily with grated cheese—Swiss or Parmesan.

● Marinate the fillets in olive or vegetable oil and lemon juice. Arrange them on skewers, sprinkle with salt, freshly ground pepper, and grated onion. Skewer and broil.

● Marinate the fillets in oil and lemon juice. Roll them in grated onion and gingerroot, season with salt and tarragon seasoning powder.

- Roll strips of partially cooked bacon around the fillets, arrange them on skewers, and broil.
- Place a piece of boiled ham and a tiny slice of dill pickle on each fillet and roll it up tightly. Fasten with a toothpick. Skewer, dip in melted butter, and broil.

Oysters

Oysters should first be just barely puffed in boiling water. Cook by any of the following methods:

- String oysters on skewers, season with salt and freshly ground pepper, dip into melted butter or bacon fat, and broil.
- Season the oysters, dip them in melted fat, and roll in dry bread or cracker crumbs. String on skewers and broil.
- Season the oysters, dip in melted fat, and roll them in crumbs to which you have added grated Parmesan cheese, chopped parsley, and a little garlic. String on skewers and broil.
- Season the oysters, dip them in melted butter seasoned with curry powder, chopped onion, and garlic. Then roll them in crumbs mixed with a little additional curry powder. String on skewers and broil.
- Roll each oyster in a small piece of partially cooked bacon; skewer and broil.
- Dip the oysters in melted butter, roll them in grated Parmesan cheese, and alternate the oysters on skewers with pieces of ham. Broil.

Barbecued Oysters and Clams

Arrange rows of oysters and clams on skewers and soak in a barbecue sauce (pages 199–204) for 2 hours. Broil quickly over charcoal or in the electric grill.

To serve: Remove oysters and clams from skewers and accompany with Spicy Sauce for Barbecued Seafood (below).

Spicy Sauce for Barbecued Seafood

1 cup dairy sour cream	1 tablespoon chopped
1 cup mayonnaise	fresh tarragon or
2 cloves garlic, crushed	1 teaspoon dried
¼ cup chopped parsley	tarragon
1 teaspoon salt	1 teaspoon dry mustard
1 tablespoon	1 teaspoon paprika
Worcestershire sauce	

Combine all ingredients and blend well.

Makes 2 cups sauce.

Shrimp

● Marinate giant shrimp in a barbecue sauce (pages 199–204). Skewer them, shell and all, and broil, basting with the sauce. They will take about 5 minutes to cook. Serve with the sauce and pass around plenty of large paper napkins.

● Shell raw shrimp, wrap each one in a piece of partially cooked bacon, and alternate them on skewers with black olives. Broil.

● Alternate shelled shrimp on skewers with small tomatoes or tomato wedges. Dip in melted fat, season with salt and freshly ground pepper, and dust with chopped parsley and grated garlic. Broil, basting with more melted fat.

● Marinate shelled raw shrimp in melted butter and oil seasoned with curry powder and chopped garlic. Roll in curry powder, season with salt and freshly ground pepper, run them on skewers, and broil.

● Alternate shelled raw shrimp on skewers with oysters (barely plumped in boiling water) and scallops. Season and brush with melted butter. Broil.

● Use shelled raw shrimp and scallops alternated on skewers, season, dip in melted butter, and then roll in crumbs. Broil and serve with a hot sauce.

123

Barbecued Shrimp I

Select jumbo shrimp—those that run 10 to 15 per pound—and shell them. String them on small skewers and marinate in a barbecue sauce (pages 199–204) for 1 hour. Broil over charcoal or in the electric grill for 3 to 5 minutes, turning once or twice during the cooking. Make a sauce to dunk them in of soy sauce, finely chopped onion and gingerroot, and a little grated horseradish.

Barbecued Shrimp II

Shell and marinate the shrimp as above, but do not skewer. When the shrimp are removed from the marinade, roll them in sesame seeds which have been toasted in a skillet, stirring constantly, until browned. Skewer and broil. The flavor is delectable.

Lobster

Barbecued Lobster

Cut the meat from cooked lobster tails in thin chunks. Arrange these on small skewers. Marinate in a barbecue sauce (pages 199–204) for 2 hours and cook very quickly over charcoal or under the electric grill.

Scallops

Scallops should be cooked only until just done, less than 5 minutes. If overcooked, they are tough. They may be grilled using any of the following methods.

• Dip scallops in melted butter, season with salt and freshly ground pepper and a dash of lemon juice. Broil on skewers until just lightly browned.

- Wrap scallops in pieces of partially cooked bacon, skewer, and broil.
- Dip scallops in melted butter, season, and roll in curry powder. Add a dash of lemon juice and broil on skewers.
- Marinate scallops in olive oil seasoned with soy sauce, lemon juice, and grated garlic. Broil on skewers, brushing with the marinade.

JAPANESE DISHES

Many Japanese recipes lend themselves readily to outdoor and indoor barbecue cooking units. They are a delightful change and fun to do for guests. Always serve them with a big bowl of rice. If you can buy the wooden rice bowls from Japan, they are attractive, relatively unbreakable, and will keep the rice hot for a long time.

To be truly authentic, most Japanese dishes call for long rice, which is really a gelantinous type of noodle (*shirataki*) that is cooked right in the meat dishes. It does not take the place of the bowl of rice and bears no resemblance to it. You may have to shop around to find this as well as the bean curd (it comes canned and dried as well as fresh) used in many Oriental dishes.

Barbecued Beef Teriyaki
This can be a main course or you can use it for a hot snack with drinks.

2 pounds sirloin or tenderloin steak
Teriyaki Sauce (page 126)

Cut the steak into thin strips and marinate in the Teriyaki Sauce for 2 hours. (Make smaller strips for hors d'oeuvres than for main course.) String the meat on skewers or wet bamboo sticks and grill it over charcoal

125

or under a broiler just long enough to sear on all sides. Baste with the sauce during the cooking.

Serves 4 as a main course or 8 as an hors d'oeuvre.

Teriyaki Sauce

½ cup Japanese soy sauce (**shoyu**)	3 tablespoons sugar
2 tablespoons sherry	2 teaspoons grated gingerroot
	1 clove garlic, grated

Combine all ingredients and blend well.

Makes about ½ cup sauce.

Barbecued Chicken Teriyaki

2 chickens (2 pounds each), boned
Teriyaki Sauce (above)

Cut the chicken into bite-sized pieces and marinate in the Teriyaki Sauce for 1 or 2 hours. Broil on wet bamboo sticks or in a hinged grill until nicely browned and cooked through. Baste with the sauce.

Serves 4 as a main course or 8 as an hors d'oeuvre.

Barbecued Spareribs Teriyaki

2 pounds spareribs
Teriyaki Sauce (above)

Parboil the spareribs for 25 minutes and then marinate in the sauce for an hour or so. Broil over charcoal until nicely browned, crisp, and cooked through. Baste with the sauce. Parboiling the spareribs first saves cooking time at the grill and cuts down on the fat.

Serves 2 as a main course or 4 as an hors d'oeuvre.

Sukiyaki

This is a quick dish to make and is spectacular and delicious.

1½ pounds sirloin or tenderloin of beef

2 or 3 strips beef fat

2 medium onions, thinly sliced

2 tablespoons sugar

½ cup Japanese soy sauce (**shoyu**)

¼ cup sherry

1 cup sliced canned bamboo shoots

12 large mushrooms, thinly sliced

½ cup beef stock or 1 bouillon cube dissolved in ½ cup hot water

2 large bunches watercress or 1 pound spinach, sliced crosswise

10 to 12 green onions or scallions, cut in small pieces

1 package long rice* (shirataki), soaked 30 minutes in warm water

1 cup or more cubed (1 inch) bean curd

¼ teaspoon monosodium glutamate

Cooked white rice

6 eggs

Slice the meat paper thin in 2x3-inch strips. Heat two medium-sized skillets or one jumbo-sized one and rub well with the beef fat until oiled. When they are smoking hot, add a little of the sliced onion and stir it around to prevent browning. Add the meat strips and sear on both sides. Add the sugar, soy sauce, and sherry. Let the liquid come to a boil and add the rest of the onion, the bamboo shoots, and the mushrooms and cook for a few minutes. Add the broth, all the greens, and the long rice.

When the long rice is just transparent, which will take a very short time, add the bean curd and monosodium glutamate. Blend all the ingredients well but do not

*If you can't find this gelatinous type of noodle, substitute vermicelli, if you wish.

overcook. The vegetables should still be crisp and bitey.

To serve: Give each person a plate for the *sukiyaki* and white rice and a small bowl into which he can break a raw egg. The egg should be stirred a bit with chop sticks. Each mouthful of *sukiyaki* is dipped into the raw egg and then eaten with the rice.

Serves 6.

Variation

Many other vegetables can be used in this dish. Thinly sliced bean sprouts, green pepper, tomato wedges, shredded carrot, thin strips of turnip—almost anything you can think of may be added or used as a substitute for the vegetables listed.

Chicken Sukiyaki

Simply substitute strips of tender chicken flesh for the beef in the preceding recipe.

Matsu Kage Yaki

This is one version of Japanese broiled chicken.

1 chicken (2½ pounds), boned	2 tablespoons grated gingerroot
½ cup Japanese soy sauce (**shoyu**)	½ teaspoon monosodium glutamate
½ cup sherry	Sesame seeds
3 tablespoons sugar	

Cut the chicken into thin strips. Combine the remaining ingredients, except the sesame seeds, and marinate the chicken strips for 2 hours. When you are ready to broil the chicken, roll each piece in sesame seeds and broil on skewers over charcoal until nicely browned and cooked through.

Serves 3 to 4.

Beef Hibachi

These are very popular cocktail snacks in Hawaii and on the Pacific coast, where they are cooked and served

*on tiny bamboo skewers. Small wooden or steel ones
will do as well.*

Use good tender beef—sirloin or the best grade of rump
steak—and cut the meat into 1½-inch strips. Then cut
each strip into paper-thin slices, marinate in Hibachi
Marinade (page 212) for about 2 hours, and string
these on skewers. Broil over charcoal for seconds only.
The heat should just curl the edges of the meat, crisp
it a bit, and give it a glaze. If you have more than one
charcoal cooker, you can let your guests do their own
grilling. Simply pass a platter of the marinated meat
on skewers and let them cook their own to taste.

To serve: Have plenty of thin slices of buttered bread
—rye, French, pumpernickel, or Armenian bread—
and slip the bits of meat off the skewers onto it. Pass
bowls of hot mustard and Chinese sweet-and-sour
sauce (page 205) for guests to select as condiments.

Pork Hibachi

Pork needs long cooking, so it is wiser to use pork that
has been pre-roasted for this dish. Cut it into 1-inch
squares sliced as thin as possible. String these on small
skewers and marinate for 2 hours in Hibachi Marinade
(page 212). They will heat through in a few minutes
in the broiler or over charcoal.

Chicken Hibachi

Cut pieces of raw chicken breast into thin strips and
thread them on small skewers. Marinate in Hibachi
Marinade (page 212) or Shish Kebab Marinade III
(page 211) for 2 hours. Broil over choarcoal or in an
electric grill for about 2 to 5 minutes, or until the
chicken is just heated through and glazed.

To serve: Pass bowls of hot mustard or chutney to
dip the chicken in.

SKILLET DISHES

Electric skillets make possible a kind of cooking and serving which is similar to the Japanese *hibachi*-top or table-top style of skillet cooking. In the chapter on "Grilling and Broiling," you'll find a number of recipes for pan-fried and sautéed dishes which can also, of course, be cooked in the electric skillet or in a cast-iron or cast-aluminum skillet over a *hibachi* or other indoor or outdoor cooking unit. The following recipes are especially good party dishes for preparation in the electric skillet or any other big, deep skillet with a cover over an open fire.

Arroz con Pollo

This is a delicious chicken and rice dish that can be found throughout Latin and South America, for it is also a favorite in Spain. Its variations are as infinite as the cooks who prepare it. Chorizos, saffron, and a garnish of green peas are often added. This is a Mexican version.

1	chicken (3 pounds)	2	teaspoons Kitchen Bouquet
2	tablespoons olive oil		
½	cup finely diced onion	½	cup sliced pimento-stuffed olives
½	cup finely diced green pepper	1	can (3 ounces) chopped broiled mushrooms (with juices)
¼	pound ham, finely diced		
1½	teaspoons salt		
¼	teaspoon freshly ground pepper	½	cup tomato sauce
		2	cups water
½	teaspoon paprika	1	cup converted rice

Cut the chicken into serving pieces. Heat the olive oil in a skillet with cover over moderate heat. Add the onion, green pepper, and ham. Cook about 5 minutes, stirring frequently. Sprinkle with the seasonings and

Kitchen Bouquet. Add the olives and contents of the can of mushrooms. Blend together and add the tomato sauce and water. Mix well and bring to the boil. Arrange the chicken pieces skin-side-down in the skillet. Cover and cook slowly for 15 minutes. Remove chicken pieces. Stir in rice and replace chicken skin-side-up. Cover and continue cooking slowly until rice is just tender, about 20 minutes longer.

Serves 4.

Chicken Cacciatori

1 chicken (3 to 3½ pounds) Seasoned flour	1 large tomato, peeled and quartered
2 tablespoons shortening	1 cup tomato sauce
1 medium onion, chopped	½ cup water
1 green pepper, chopped	2 tablespoons dry white wine
½ sweet red pepper, chopped	1 tablespoon salt
1 clove garlic, minced	⅛ teaspoon freshly ground pepper

Cut the chicken into serving pieces. Dredge in seasoned flour. Preheat a skillet with cover to between medium and high heat. Melt shortening and brown chicken on all sides. Combine the remaining ingredients and pour over chicken. Reduce heat, cover, and simmer until done, adding liquid if necessary. Serve hot from the skillet.

Serves 4.

Veal Scallopini

1½	pounds veal round, thinly sliced	1	cup chicken stock or bouillon
	Seasoned flour	½	cup dry white wine
1	tablespoon butter	¼	cup tomato juice
1	tablespoon olive oil	⅛	teaspoon nutmeg
1	clove garlic, sliced	¼	cup grated
1	small onion, sliced		Parmesan cheese
1	can (4 ounces) mushrooms	2	tablespoons chopped parsley

Preheat a skillet with cover to a little above medium. Trim skin and gristle from veal. Dredge in seasoned flour and pound thin. Cut into 1x3-inch strips. Melt butter, add oil, and sauté garlic and onion. Brown veal on both sides. Remove garlic and add mushrooms, chicken stock, wine, tomato juice and nutmeg.

Reduce heat to below medium. Cover and cook 30 minutes, or until done, stirring occasionally. Add more liquid if necessary. Sprinkle with cheese, cover, and let stand about 10 minutes before serving.

To serve: Garnish with chopped parsley and ladle hot from the skillet.

Serves 4.

Carbonnade Flamande

2	pounds onions, sliced		Salt and freshly ground
	Butter or beef fat		pepper to taste
	Flour	2	cloves garlic
3	pounds chuck steak	2	cups dark beer

Sauté onions in butter until soft and lightly browned. You will need about 5 tablespoons of butter for this—or you can use beef fat. Meanwhile, cube, flour, and brown the chuck steak very quickly in 3 tablespoons of fat. When it is nicely browned, combine it with the onions in a Dutch oven or deep kettle and add the salt and pepper, garlic, and beer. Cover and simmer for approximately 1¼ hours, or until tender. Add a little flour and butter kneaded together and stir until the stew thickens slightly. Taste for seasoning and serve at once.

To serve: Plenty of boiled potatoes or a great baked potato, crisp bread, and beer to drink are traditional accompaniments for this dish.

Serves 6.

PICNICS, BIG PARTY DISHES, & CLAMBAKES

PICNICS

I was brought up in a household famous for its fabulous cooking, and the memories of my childhood are full of one fine meal after another. But the most exciting of all were the magnificent family picnics. Huge hampers and baskets were filled with an endless array of delectable tidbits to be consumed in the great outdoors—on a wide sandy beach by the Pacific, or high in the mountains where blue and red huckleberries grew in abundance, or along some winding road deep in a canyon beside a rushing stream.

For the cold food and drink, we stopped at an ice house and picked up a large cake of ice which sat on the floor in the back of the car with the perishables on top. If we wanted anything hot, and we usually planned on coffee at least, we'd build a fire in the open, or if we were near woods that might catch from a fire, we'd manage with a little alcohol stove.

Equipment

Today's picnicker has no such problems. He can take along a small portable cooking grill that is easy to set up and use. Some bucket-shaped grills have handles and serve as containers to carry their own charcoal or briquets, or some of your picnic supplies. They take little or no room in the back seat or the trunk compartment. Then there is the old reliable portable gasoline stove, the Coleman, which has served campers and outdoor enthusiasts for years. For heating coffee or soup, a little folding Sterno stove can be used wherever you stop. And if you're heading for one of the wayside picnic groves that are found along many of our great highways, you can usually find an outdoors fireplace. You'll need only a hinged basket grill and whatever other equipment your cooking plans will call for. You'll do well to carry along your own kindling, charcoal, and firewood, unless you're sure such supplies are available at your chosen spot.

Carrying hot or cold food and drink is a simple matter today. There are small portable ice boxes which will hold about 12 pounds of ice, and large thermos jugs for hot or cold food or drink. Or you can use one of the handy bucket coolers packed with ice cubes and your food and it will keep cold for hours. It's a good idea to take along some hot coffee in a thermos bottle or jug, even though you plan to cook a fresh pot of it at the picnic site. Then you won't have to wait for your first cup until after the food is off the grill. And naturally you'll want to carry it that way if you're not sure of being able to find cooking facilities at your picnic site.

If you use paper plates and cups for serving, be sure they're the kind that don't get soggy. Plastic dishes are much more serviceable, though of course not so easily disposable. If you do any amount of picnicking, it will be worth your while to invest in one of those wonderful picnic baskets that are equipped with a thermos bottle or two, plastic dishes, stainless steel cutlery, and salt and pepper shakers, all held in place and with room left for sandwiches and other supplies. You might also look into the many sets of portable cooking equipment designed for campers and for the use of the armed forces, available respectively at sporting-good stores and surplus dealers.

In planning your picnic meals, you'll do well to plan a simple menu of hearty grub that will satisfy appetites sharpened by fresh air and the tang of woodsmoke. Stick to three or four items, have them of the best quality, and serve plenty of 'em.

Picnic Food

This whole book is packed with recipes and suggestions that will lend themselves beautifully to picnic planning. Hamburgers and frankfurters, which are top-ranking picnic fare, will be found on pages 31–39. On pages 154–158 you will find a selection of grilled sandwiches that will round out the sandwich suggestions here. For tips on coffee-making, good outdoors drinks, and many other ingredients of great eating in the open, thumb through this book in both directions, and see how easily you can adapt many of the suggestions to your picnicking.

One classic dish for a picnic is fried chicken, cooked beforehand and reheated or eaten cold. It has superb flavor and goes wonderfully well with the other traditional picnic foods: Stuffed eggs, potato salad, baked beans, and chocolate cake. Here are two popular ways to cook fried chicken, followed by good accompaniments and other picnic favorites.

Southern Fried Chicken

Heat fat in your electric or other deep-fat fryer to 370°F. Dip serving-size pieces of chicken in flour seasoned with salt and pepper and fry for 12 to 15 minutes, or until the chicken is golden brown. Let the chicken pieces cool and drain on absorbent paper. Wrap each piece separately in foil or waxed paper.

Old-Fashioned Fried Chicken

Pour olive oil in a skillet until it reaches a depth of 1 inch. Heat the oil and dip the chicken pieces in seasoned flour and then brown them quickly on all sides in the hot oil. Turn the heat down slightly and let the chicken cook until it is tender. This should take about 25 to 28 minutes. Drain and cool the chicken. Wrap each piece separately in foil or waxed paper.

Baked Beans

When I was a child, I would have been amazed to see anyone open a can of pork and beans at a picnic, for we always brought along a huge pan of homemade baked beans, made with salt pork, onion, and mustard, and a very little brown sugar. Too much sweet spoils the flavor of baked beans, to my mind. My mother's baked beans were famous all over the beach colony. Here is how she made them:

Soak 1 pound of white pea beans overnight. In the morning put them to cook in salted water—more than enough to cover them. Add an onion stuck with 2 cloves and a bay leaf. Let the beans simmer until soft but not mushy. Drain them and save the cooking water.

Place a layer of beans in a large casserole, cover it with thin slices of salt pork and onion, add another layer of beans, and sprinkle it with dry mustard. Now add a layer of garlic sausage, salami, or summer sausage, another layer of sliced onions, more dry mustard, and just a sprinkling of brown sugar. Top with a layer of beans and cover with slices of salt pork. Pour the liquid from cooking the beans over this and bake it at 300°F. for 2 or 3 hours, adding more water if it gets too dry.

Serves 8.

Sandwiches

Sandwiches, like many other everyday foods, are often treated carelessly. They can make wonderful outdoors meals if prepared properly with the best ingredients. The major consideration is the bread. Don't use the cottony, thick-sliced white type that is so widely sold. The best sandwiches are made of very thin slices of firm bread and plenty of tasty filling. If you can't get bread of good, firm texture at your grocery store, search the neighborhood for those long, thin loaves of French bread. Or find a bakery where you can get good home-made-style bread, hearth-baked bread, or rye bread.

Have your butter soft so it will spread evenly. Sometimes a little flavor added to the butter makes the sandwich tastier. Try adding a little garlic to the butter for meat fillings, a little lemon and parsley for fish fillings, mustard—prepared or dry—for ham or chicken, and curry whenever you like it.

Spread the bread well with the butter and top it with plenty of filling. Cover with another slice of bread, press down firmly, and either cut in two pieces or leave whole. Wrap each sandwich separately in foil or waxed paper. Put them in the refrigerator to chill. This always makes them better.

If the fillings you have selected tend to make the bread soggy, carry them in separate containers and assemble your sandwiches on the site of your picnic.

Here are some suggestions for fillings:

- Thinly sliced Italian or Bermuda onions sprinkled with salt.
- Thinly sliced cucumber with mayonnaise.
- Thin slices of chicken with mayonnaise.
- Thin slices of rare roast beef with mustard butter.
- Thin slices of old-fashioned baked ham (not the boiled ham sold in most groceries) with mustard or chutney.
- Club sandwich: Toast slices of bread. On the bottom slice spread butter, then mayonnaise, then place a piece of lettuce, top it with sliced tomato, sliced chicken, and

cooked crisp bacon. Add more mayonnaise and top with the other slice of toast. Press together and wrap in foil.

● Chopped cooked chicken livers and chopped egg, mixed together, seasoned with onion, and moistened with chicken fat or mayonnaise.
● Chopped shrimp, seasoned with a bit of onion and parsley and moistened with mayonnaise.
● Lobster tail thinly sliced, seasoned with salt and pepper, and spread with mayonnaise.
● Chopped egg, pickle, and mayonnaise.
● Head cheese.
● Cream cheese, sliced stuffed olives, and onion.
● Cream cheese, smoked salmon, and onion.
● Corned beef, sliced pickle, and onion.
● Cold roast lamb with pickle relish and curry butter.
● Cold sliced steak with mustard.
● Slices of Swiss cheese with mustard.
● Ham and Swiss cheese.
● Tongue and mustard.
● Tongue, cheese, and horseradish.

Cooking in Foil

Aluminum foil is an invaluable accessory when you're cooking in the great outdoors. You can wrap potatoes in foil and roast them in the ashes of your picnic fire. You can treat apples in the same manner. Almost any fruit or vegetable that is good baked can be cooked this way.

Lobsters are excellent when wrapped in foil before broiling or grilling. The foil keeps the shells from getting too scorched and an extra thickness around the claws protects them from overcooking. Small fish and fillets—any delicate fish—seasoned, brushed with butter, and rolled in foil will cook beautifully directly on the hot coals. Larger fish with tougher skin are better broiled on a grill without the foil, as they need to be crispy on the outside.

Ready-cooked meat dishes with sauces can be packed

for your picnic and reheated in foil right on the coals. Simply unfold the foil wrapping of your dish and form it into a cuplike container which can be bedded into the hot ashes.

You can use foil for cooling as well as heating. Wrap your salad greens or fruit, or whatever you wish to cool in foil, and put them in a running stream or lake. Or if you're not planning to picnic near a stream, put some ice cubes in a covered pan with your foil-wrapped greens. The foil will keep the greens from getting soggy as the ice melts.

BIG PARTY DISHES

Brunswick stew and Burgoo are two favorite dishes for outdoor parties in the South. They are made in huge quantities for barbecues and gatherings in the countryside, and make for really wonderful eating wherever they are served. Here's how to make a Brunswick stew:

Brunswick Stew

1	fowl (7 to 8 pounds)	1	tablespoon salt
3	pounds beef shin or bottom round	1	bay leaf
2	squirrels or rabbits	1	onion stuck with cloves
2	pounds veal neck bones	1	tablespoon freshly ground pepper
		9	quarts water

Combine the meats with the seasonings and water and bring to a boil. Skim, cover, and reduce the heat. Simmer until the meat is practically falling from the bones, about 2 hours or more. Strain off the broth and add to it:

3 pounds lima beans, shelled	1 or 2 ripe tomatoes, coarsely chopped
12 small white onions	
24 medium potatoes, peeled	2 large bunches celery, finely sliced
12 ears corn, kernels only	2 pounds okra, finely sliced

Cook until the vegetables are tender. Remove the meat from the bones and cut into pieces. Discard the bones. Add the meat to the vegetables and season with:

1 cup tomato puree	3 red chili peppers, seeded and chopped
½ pound butter	
2 cups red wine	⅛ teaspoon cayenne pepper
6 tablespoons sugar	
1 tablespoon salt	Dash or two of Tabasco sauce

Cook for several hours over a low flame until well blended. Stir from time to time from the bottom of the kettle. Just before serving (this is not strictly traditional) add:

2 pounds freshly cooked green beans
2 pounds freshly cooked peas
Chopped parsley

To serve: This dish calls for large bowls and plenty of cornbread or crisp French bread. Red wine or beer is the appropriate accompaniment.

Serves at least 24.

Kentucky Burgoo

2	pounds shoulder of veal	3	pounds lean breast of lamb
1	veal knuckle or 2 pounds veal neck bones	1	fowl (6 pounds)
		1	soup bone
		8	quarts water
2	pounds loin of pork		Salt
2	pounds beef shin		Freshly ground pepper

Combine all ingredients with the water and seasonings. Let the water come to a boil and boil for 5 minutes. Skim. Cover and simmer until the meat is tender, about 2 hours or more. Cool the meat, chop it rather coarsely, and discard the bones. Combine with:

2	pounds small potatoes, peeled	4	cups whole-kernel corn
2	pounds small white onions	2	chili peppers, seeded and chopped
12	carrots	1	pound okra, diced
3	green peppers, seeded and cut in strips	2	cups lima beans, parboiled
1	medium head cabbage, coarsely shredded	1	large bunch celery, coarsely chopped
		4	cups chopped tomatoes
		2	cups tomato puree

Combine all the vegetables with the meat and broth and cover. Simmer until it is almost a soup. Season with:

1	tablespoon salt or more	1	tablespoon dry mustard
			Tabasco sauce
1	tablespoon freshly ground pepper		to taste
		¼	teaspoon cayenne pepper

Stir the stew frequently with a large paddle and let it cook slowly for several hours until perfectly blended and flavored. Just before serving add generous amounts of:

Chopped parsley
Chopped green onions

To serve: Accompany the stew with plenty of crisp hot bread or biscuits and beer.

Serves at least 24.

Clam Chowder for a Big Party

1	pound bacon, cut in small pieces	1	teaspoon salt
1	pound onions, finely chopped		Freshly ground pepper to taste
1	tablespoon chopped green pepper	4	cups milk, scalded
1½	pounds potatoes, peeled and finely diced	2	cups light cream, scalded
3	cups boiling clam juice or water (use reserved clam liquor and add enough bottled clam juice or water to make 3 cups)	2	quarts clams, shucked or steamed open (reserve clam liquor)
			Chopped parsley
			Thyme

Try out the bacon in a large kettle. Add the onion and the chopped pepper and cook for just a few minutes, until slightly colored and soft. Add the potatoes and the clam juice and cook until the potatoes are just tender. Season with salt and pepper. Add the scalded milk and cream and bring just to the boiling point. Add the clams and cook just long enough to heat them through.

To serve: Dust with chopped parsley and a sprinkling of thyme. Serve in large bowls with plenty of big chowder crackers. After this hearty dish you might serve a few broiled frankfurters, or a hearty dessert.

This soup is also good to have around for lingering

cocktail parties. Let the guests serve it to themselves in mugs and have on hand an array of sausages and cold meats with a selection of good breads to accompany them.

Serves 12 to 16.

Spaghetti and Meat Sauce for a Big Party

Finely chop or grind:

1	small bunch celery	6	leeks
8	cloves garlic	1	small bunch parsley
8	medium onions	1	cup pine nuts

Sauté these ingredients in ¼ pound butter until just heated through. Toss around a little and add salt and freshly ground pepper to taste. Add:

1	pound mushrooms, sliced	1½	teaspoons salt
2½	pounds loin of pork	6	cups thick tomato puree
3	pounds beef top round	2	cups broth or canned consommé
1	tablespoon or more sweet basil		

Bring to a boil and simmer for 1 hour or until the meat is tender and cooked through. Remove the meat and let the sauce cook down slowly for 1½ hours. Remove the meat from the bones and either serve the sauce with the meat in thin slices or grind the meat and return to the sauce.

To cook spaghetti:
One pound will serve four persons. Cook the spaghetti in plenty of boiling salted water until it is just tender —do not let it get mushy. Drain and steam for a moment.

To serve: Dish up the spaghetti and pour some sauce over each portion. Plenty of grated Parmesan or Romano cheese is an absolute necessity—served in bowls and added by your guests according to their tastes.

Serves about 18 to 20.

Chili for a Big Party

5 pounds onions, finely chopped	½ cup peanut oil or olive oil
¼ pound butter	6 pounds beef top round, cubed or chopped

Sauté the onions in the combined fats until they are soft but not colored. Add the beef and brown it very quickly with the onions. Add:

1⅛ tablespoons salt	1½ teaspoons oregano
4 cloves garlic, finely chopped	4 cups tomato puree
	2 cups tomato juice
6 tablespoons chili powder	2 small red chili peppers, seeded and chopped
1 tablespoon cumin	

Let simmer very slowly for 2 hours, adding more tomato juice if the mixture becomes too thick for your taste. Taste for seasoning—you may want it hotter or more pungent.

To serve: This dish should be presented in bowls with crackers, or with red beans, fried beans, or rice —or as a spaghetti sauce or over frankfurters. Beer is a necessity.

Serves about 18.

Chicken with Green Molé Sauce

1	large fowl (about 6 pounds)	6	hot green chili peppers
1	onion stuck with 2 cloves	1	cup chopped parsley Olive oil
2	teaspoons salt Freshly ground pepper to taste		Chopped cilantro or cardamom or parsley sprigs
½	cup pumpkin seeds		

Clean and cut the chicken as for a fricassee—the legs, thighs, back pieces, and wings cut separately and the breast cut into two or three pieces. Put all the pieces, except the breast, into a pot with just enough water to cover. Add the onion, salt, and pepper and bring to a boil. Cover and reduce the heat and simmer for 1 hour. Add the breast and continue simmering until the chicken is tender.

Toast the pumpkin seeds until they are crisp and delicately brown. Pierce the peppers with a fork and hold them over a flame until they blister and the skin loosens. Remove the skin and the seeds and grind or chop the peppers with the pumpkin seeds. The seeds and peppers must make a paste—pound in a mortar or put through a food mill after chopping. Add the chopped parsley and heat the mixture in preheated oil.

Pour the broth from the chicken and measure and reduce until you have just 2 cups. Add this to the mixture in the pan, heat thoroughly, pour over the chicken, and simmer for about 10 minutes.

To serve: Garnish with cilantro or cardamon or with parsley sprigs. Serve with rice.

Serves 6 to 8.

NOTE: You can simplify this recipe by using canned green molé sauce (available from Mexican stores). Merely follow the directions for amount on the can and heat the sauce in olive oil with additional chopped

parsley and reduced broth. Pour the sauce over the
chicken before serving.

Turkey with Molé Sauce

*Here is another molé which takes a long time to prepare
but is worth the trouble. The result is a big stewy job
which you can serve with fried beans for a truly good
meal.*

Cut up a 12-pound turkey into serving-size pieces which
will fit into a large kettle. Cover with water and add
1 large onion stuck with cloves, 2 cloves garlic, 1 bay
leaf, and a bit of oregano. Simmer until the turkey is
tender—this depends upon the age of the bird.

While it is simmering prepare these three different
types of chili peppers (these and the tortillas you will
need may be bought canned in Mexican shops):

30 mulatos chilies   15 pasilla chilies
25 anchos chilies

Toast the chilies over a flame for a few minutes and
soak in water, after removing the skin and seeds. Combine with:

2 toasted tortillas   ½ pound toasted almonds
1 large onion   ¼ cup sesame seed
3 cloves garlic   2 ounces unsweetened
¼ teaspoon cardamon   chocolate

Grind the above ingredients exceedingly fine and add:

1½ quarts turkey broth   ½ teaspoon cumin seed
    (from the turkey)   1 tablespoon salt
1   teaspoon freshly
    ground pepper

Heat this mixture to the boiling point and pour over the
turkey. Rinse the pan with a little more broth, pour
over the turkey, and let it simmer for an hour.

To serve: Garnish with black olives and toasted

147

almonds and serve with fried beans and toasted tortillas.

Serves 16 to 20.

Mexican Fried Beans

This dish—frijoles—*is a mainstay of the Mexican menu and a delicious addition to your barbecue-cooking repertoire. Since beans have about as much protein as meat, you can serve* frijoles *as a hearty main dish, with a salad on the side. It's a good dish to make in quantity for a large crowd—or to store and serve again as* frijoles refritos—*refried beans.*

Wash 1 pound of pink beans (if you can't get them, use pinto beans). Put them on to cook with 2 quarts of water and an onion stuck with 2 cloves. Add a tablespoon of salt and let them cook until soft but not mushy (test them now and then while cooking).

In a heavy pot, put about ⅓ pound of lard (for the authentic Mexican flavor), or bacon or chicken fat if you prefer. When it is melted, add some of the beans and mash them down well. Then add some of the bean liquor and repeat this process until all the beans are used up. Don't mash as thoroughly as you would potatoes; leave some of the beans whole and others mashed. Serve as is, thick and delectable.

For *frijoles refritos* you simply heat some fat in your skillet and fry the beans again, crushing and stirring them and letting them get really crusty and wonderful.

Serves 10 to 12.

Black Bean Casserole

Soak 2 pounds of black beans overnight. Pour this water off the next morning and cover to 1 inch above beans with fresh water. Add 1 onion stuck with 2 cloves, a bay leaf, and 2 garlic cloves and cook until the beans are tender. Remove the beans to a casserole, strain the liquid, and combine with ½ cup of dark rum and ½ cup of tomato puree. Pour this over the beans and top with thin slices of salt pork which have been parboiled for 30 minutes. Bake in a preheated oven at 350°F. until the salt pork is nicely browned and cooked through and the beans well blended.

To serve: These beans go well with pork dishes and with such game dishes as duck and pheasant. *Serves 12.*

CLAMBAKES

New England Clambake

This is a classic New England shore feast. It takes time to prepare and should be planned well in advance. Arrange to do it when you are going to spend the whole day at the beach. For a clambake for 20 people, start by digging a shallow hole in the ground, about 10 to 12 inches deep and about a yard across. Line the hole with rocks. Try to get flattish oval rocks that are smooth, if you can. Build a huge fire with kindling and hardwood to cover the whole surface of the rocks, and keep it going until the rocks are thoroughly heated, so that they sizzle and steam when water is dripped on them. This will take some hours.

Now you rake away all the fire and ashes and brush the rocks clean. Hurry this job so they won't cool off. Add a layer of wet setweed several inches deep. Spread wire mesh over the seaweed and cover this with softshell clams, washed and scrubbed. You will need about ⅔ of a bushel of clams for 20 people. Top the clams with one live lobster per person, and put on a final layer of some vegetable—either corn in its husks or whole unpeeled potatoes. Cover the whole pile with a large sheet of canvas to hold in the steam. The canvas must be weighted down around the edges with more rocks.

This whole job must be accomplished very quickly or the rocks will cool and your clambake will be uncooked. It's no job for one person. Line up several helpers and have the food all ready to pop into the pit.

The clambake should steam at least an hour. You can test for doneness by cracking open one of the lobsters near the edge of the bake.

To go with the clambake, serve plenty of melted butter, big slabs of good bread, pickles, and cold beer. Be sure you have an ample supply of eating utensils —nutcrackers for the lobsters, forks, plastic plates, and plenty of paper napkins.

Easy-Way Clambake

This is a much simpler and more practical method for preparing a clambake. Use a large kettle. Cover the bottom of the kettle with wet seaweed. Add 1 live lobster for each person. Top with more seaweed. Put in a layer of corn in its husks. Top with another layer of seaweed and spread clams over this. Place a covering of seaweed over all, put a cover on the kettle, and let it steam over your grill for about an hour and a half. Of course the cooking time depends on how hot your fire is. But you can test by trying one of the clams.

To serve: The clams come first. Leave the kettle with the rest of its ingredients steaming while the clams are being eaten. Pass plenty of paper napkins and melted butter. When the clams are eaten, dish out the corn. Pass more butter, more paper napkins, and salt and pepper. Finally, serve the lobsters, again with paper napkins and melted butter.

Have plenty of good bread, and beer or coffee.

BREADS, PANCAKES, & BAKING

BREADS

Outdoors food calls for bread of fine flavor and robust texture. The usual grocery store bread is too soft and neutral to go well with steaks, chops, and spitted meats. Good French and Italian bread, with their crustiness and chewier texture, are ideal accompaniments for this type of food, and in some places you can also buy the incomparable sourdough bread—one of the best breads ever invented. Armenian and Balkan breads, especially *lavash*, which is flat and rather chewy, are excellent with outdoors food.

Other good kinds of bread are Russian and German ryes, different kinds of pumpernickel, Swedish hard breads, and Jewish *matzos*, bagels, and the delicious onion rolls. These last are outstanding with steak, and steak sandwich made on an onion roll is exceptional.

If your group is small enough and your grill large enough (or you have an extra one), save steps to the kitchen and heat these breads on the back of the grill. Otherwise, serve hot from the oven. Flavored and wrapped loaves or rolls can be carried to the picnic site and warmed there.

Any of the following flavored butters may be used with French or Italian hard rolls split and prepared the same way. This may be more advantageous for a large party.

Herbed Breads

Garlic Bread

Use French or Italian bread. Rub the loaf well with a clove of garlic until the flavor has penetrated the crust. Split the loaf the long way and toast it over the coals, or wrap it in aluminum foil and put it on the least warm spot of the grill to heat gradually. If you are using an oven, heat at 350°F. for about 15 minutes.

Buttered Garlic Bread

Slice a long French or Italian loaf in slices, cutting just to the bottom crust, but not right through. Melt ¼ pound of butter with 2 grated cloves of garlic. Let the butter absorb the garlic flavor thoroughly. Fan the slices of bread apart and pour a little of the garlic butter in between each 2 slices. Brush the top with the garlic butter. Heat the loaf in a 350°F. oven for 15 minutes, or wrap it in foil and heat on the back of your grill.

Herbed Rye Bread

Take a loaf of thinly sliced sour rye and spread each slice with garlic-flavored butter and sprinkle each slice with finely chopped parsley and a hint of dried thyme or rosemary. Place the slices together, loaf-fashion, wrap in foil, and heat on the back of the grill or bake at 375°F. for 15 to 20 minutes, or until the butter is thoroughly melted and the herb flavor is blended.

Herbed French Bread

This is my favorite way to fix bread. It makes a wonderful accompaniment to any outdoor meal and is good enough to be served by itself as an appetizer.

1 loaf French or Italian bread	¼ cup chopped green onions
¼ pound butter, softened	¼ cup chopped chives or 2 cloves garlic, finely chopped
1 cup chopped parsley	

Cut the loaf of bread the long way. Mix the remaining ingredients and spread on the two halves of the loaf. Put the bread back together, sandwich fashion, and wrap in foil. Heat on the back of the grill or bake in the oven at 350°F. for about 15 minutes.

Herbed Loaf

1 bunch green onions, chopped	1 teaspoon dry mustard
½ cup chopped parsley	½ pound butter, softened
2 tablespoons chopped fresh basil	1 long French loaf or 2 round Italian loaves

Mix the green onions, parsley, basil, and mustard with the butter. Split the French bread down the length or the Italian bread through the middle and spread with the mixture. Put the bread back together again, sandwich fashion, and wrap in foil. Heat on the back of the grill or bake in the oven at 375°F. for about 15 minutes.

Mustard Bread

½ pound butter, softened
1 cup finely chopped green onions
½ cup chopped parsley
Few drops of lemon juice

1 long loaf French or Italian bread
Prepared mustard
Toasted sesame seeds

Combine the butter, green onions, parsley, and lemon juice and cream well. Spoon onto split loaf halves. Top with mustard and sprinkle with sesame seeds. Heat on grill—or much better—in the oven, and serve hot.

Cheese Loaf

½ pound butter, softened
½ pound sharp Cheddar cheese, grated
2 teaspoons dry mustard

Dash of cayenne pepper
2 long loaves French or Italian bread

Combine the butter, cheese, mustard, and cayenne and blend well. Split the bread lengthwise and spread with the butter-cheese mixture. Press the halves together and wrap in foil. Heat on the back of the grill, turning quite often, or bake in the oven at 375°F. until the cheese is melted.

Grilled Sandwiches

As an alternative to or accompaniment for the usual burgers and frankfurters, toasted sandwiches are a good choice. When cut into finger strips, or any small sizes you wish, they make delicious canapés which your guests can prepare themselves on a smaller grill while you preside at the large outdoor grill. In either case, have the sandwiches all ready to be toasted. Here are suggestions for good combinations.

Mustard-Cheese Sandwiches or Appetizers

1 cup (4 ounces) grated   ¼ cup mayonnaise
    Swiss cheese or   1 teaspoon dry mustard
    Cheddar cheese   Dash of Tabasco sauce

Mix all ingredients well and spread on bread slices. Make sandwiches and toast.

Makes about 1 cup spread.

Toasted Cheese Sandwiches or Appetizers

Arrange sliced Cheddar or Swiss cheese between slices of bread and toast until the cheese is runny.

Spicy Cheese Sandwiches or Appetizers

1 cup (4 ounces) grated   2 tablespoons A-1 sauce
    Swiss cheese or   2 tablespoons catsup
    Cheddar cheese

Mix all ingredients well and spread on bread slices. Make sandwiches and toast.

Makes about 1 cup spread.

Ham-Cheese Sandwiches or Appetizers

1 cup (4 ounces) grated   2 tablespoons grated
    Swiss cheese or   onion
    Cheddar cheese   ¼ cup deviled ham

Mix all ingredients well and spread on bread slices. Make sandwiches and toast.

Makes about 1¼ cups spread.

Anchovy-Cream Cheese Sandwiches or Appetizers

1 package (4 ounces) cream cheese
1 egg, beaten

2 tablespoons grated onion
6 anchovy fillets, chopped

Mash the cream cheese with a fork. Beat in the egg, onion, and anchovies until well mixed. Spread on bread slices, make sandwiches, and toast.

Makes about ¾ cup spread.

Ham-Cream Cheese Sandwiches or Appetizers

1 package (4 ounces) cream cheese
1 egg, beaten
¼ cup chopped ham

1 teaspoon dry mustard
Salt and freshly ground pepper to taste

Mash the cream cheese with a fork. Beat in the remaining ingredients until well mixed. Spread on bread slices, make sandwiches, and toast.

Makes about 1 cup spread.

Pickled Cream Cheese Sandwiches or Appetizers

1 package (4 ounces) cream cheese
1 egg, beaten
2 tablespoons chopped pickle
2 tablespoons chopped onion

2 tablespoons chopped parsley
Salt and freshly ground pepper to taste

Mash the cream cheese with a fork. Beat in the remaining ingredients until well mixed. Spread on bread slices, make sandwiches, and toast.

Makes about ¾ cup spread.

Mushroom-Cream Cheese Sandwiches or Appetizers

1	package (4 ounces) cream cheese	Chopped parsley
1	egg, beaten	Salt and freshly ground pepper to taste
1	clove garlic, grated	
2	tablespoons chopped mushrooms	

Mash the cream cheese with a fork. Beat in the remaining ingredients, using enough parsley to add color, until well mixed. Spread on bread slices, make sandwiches, and toast.

Makes about ¾ cup spread.

Sardine-Cream Cheese Sandwiches or Appetizers

1	package (4 ounces) cream cheese	2	tablespoons chopped onion
1	egg, beaten	2	tablespoons lemon juice
1	sardine (boneless and skinless), mashed		

Mash the cream cheese. Beat in the remaining ingredients until well mixed. Spread on bread slices, make sandwiches, and toast.

Makes about 1 cup spread.

Grilled Italian Cheese Sandwich
This is an exceptionally tasty—and different—sandwich.

Start by spreading halves of long French or round Italian loaves lavishly with butter. Add a layer of sliced mozzarella cheese, a layer of anchovy fillets, a layer of thinly sliced onions, and a layer of chopped parsley. Press them together and wrap in aluminum foil. Heat on the back of the grill or bake unwrapped in the oven at 375°F. for 15 to 20 minutes.

PANCAKES

Pancakes are wonderful for eating in the outdoors, and they are delicious for breakfast, supper, or dessert. For easier carrying, premix the dry ingredients before you leave home. Of course, these pancakes can be cooked on your kitchen range.

Cornmeal Griddlecakes

For breakfast, I like cornmeal pancakes with plenty of syrup and butter or with sugar and lemon juice and butter. These are much like the flapjacks of the pioneer days.

½ cup flour	2 eggs
2 teaspoons baking powder	1 cup milk (approximately)
½ teaspoon salt	4 tablespoons butter, melted
1 tablespoon sugar	
2 cups water-ground cornmeal	

Sift together the flour, baking powder, salt, and sugar and combine with the cornmeal. Beat the eggs until light and lemon colored and add to the dry ingredients. Stir with enough milk to make the batter the consistency of very heavy cream. Add the melted butter, pour the batter onto a hot, well-buttered griddle, and bake until the dough bubbles. Turn and bake until well browned on the other side. Serve with any topping you choose.

Makes about 20 4-inch griddlecakes.

Sour Cream Pancakes

These are thick cakes but very light. Use plenty of butter on the griddle when baking them.

2	eggs	½	teaspoon soda
1	cup dairy sour cream	½	teaspoon salt
1¾	cups flour	¼	cup oil or
2	teaspoons baking powder		4 tablespoons butter, melted

Beat the eggs until light and lemon colored. Gradually beat in the sour cream and continue beating until well blended. Combine the flour, baking powder, soda, and salt and sift into the batter. Mix. When well blended, add the oil and beat well. Bake on a hot griddle, dropping by spoonfuls and turning when the uncooked side is bubbly.

To serve: For breakfast with butter and syrup or honey; for supper with fried apple rings, butter, and grated maple sugar.

Sour Cream Fruit Shortcakes

This makes a dessert that is absolutely fabulous.

Add 2 tablespoons sugar with the other dry ingredients to Sour Cream Pancakes (opposite). Bake as above.

To serve: Butter the pancakes well. Cover one cake with crushed sugared fruit, top with another pancake and butter and fruit, and then add cream or whipped cream or dairy sour cream.

BAKING OUTDOORS

Generally, baking outdoors is an unnecessary chore. However, if you're going on a camping trip of several days' duration and want fresh baked goods, take along a box or two of prepared mix and follow directions on the box.

If you have a way to keep things cold, use frozen breads and biscuits or other brown-and-serve prepared breads. They are very good.

Foil-Baked Biscuits

Bake a batch of biscuits as you need them in a reflector oven made in this way:

Take a 24-inch length of heavy-duty aluminum foil and bend it in the center at a 45° angle. Place on a stone or other flat surface 6 inches above the ground and close to the edge of a flaming fire. Prop up the top of the sheet of foil at each side with a forked stick. Mix biscuit dough from any good prepared mix, using water. Mixing can be done in a paper bag or a container shaped from another piece of foil.

Grease the bottom of the reflector oven slightly, shape 2-inch patties of dough, and place them on the bottom of the oven. Rub a small amount of the dry mix on the fingers before shaping the biscuits so that the dough does not stick to the fingers. Place the oven so that an intense heat is reflected into it. When the biscuits have browned on top, turn them over and continue baking for a minute or two. The whole baking operation should not take over 10 minutes with a hot fire.

Pan-Baked Bread and Cake

If you have even, moderate heat, you can bake bread, biscuits, and cake with practically any of the prepared mixes in any deep, heavy skillet with a close-fitting cover. An electric skillet can also be used.

Start by lining the skillet with three layers of waxed paper, trimming the edges so that the lid fits on tightly and securely. Prepare the mix according to directions on the package. Preheat the skillet at low-to-moderate heat, pour in the batter, cover, and bake for 45 minutes, or until done. Place plate over the skillet and invert to remove bread or cake. Remove waxed paper while bread or cake is hot.

Pan-Baked Spoon Bread

3	cups milk	½	teaspoon baking
¾	cup white cornmeal		powder
5	eggs, separated	1½	teaspoons salt
		3	tablespoons butter

Preheat skillet at moderate heat. Scald milk, add cornmeal, stirring constantly. Cook until mixture is very thick. Beat egg yolks until light. Add baking powder and salt. Add a little cornmeal mixture to yolks, then combine yolks with remaining cornmeal. Add butter (or margarine). Beat egg whites until stiff but not dry and fold in carefully. Pour into lightly greased skillet. Cover and cook 35 minutes over moderate heat without raising cover.

FROM
THE
KITCHEN

APPETIZERS
& SNACKS

Half the fun of outdoor cooking is having an audience to admire your artistry. This means that guests must wait a while for their dinner. To keep them happily occupied, serve good, hearty drinks, along with plenty of substantial appetizers. Forget the quaint little canapés that the women's magazines feature. Instead, serve something easy to fix but satisfying. Here are some suggestions for dunks.

DUNK BOWLS

Serve any raw vegetables you like: Cucumber strips, celery sticks, pepper strips, carrot sticks, cauliflowerets, asparagus tips, sliced turnips, green onions, radishes, endive, or any other favorite. Put them in a bowl with ice to keep them crisp and let each guest help himself and dip into the dunk sauce.

Mayonnaise Dunk

1½ cups mayonnaise
1 clove garlic, grated
1 hard-cooked egg, chopped
Juice of 1 lemon
Dash of tarragon seasoning powder
6 green onions, finely chopped
Heavy cream

Combine all ingredients except heavy cream and mix well. Taste for seasoning and dilute with heavy cream to dunking consistency.

Makes about 1¾ cups dunk.

Caviar Dunk

This is a very highly seasoned dunk.

½ cup soft bread crumbs
¼ cup milk
1 jar (8 ounces) red caviar
1 large onion, finely chopped
1 cup dairy sour cream

Soak the bread crumbs in the milk. Add the crumbs with the caviar and onion to the jar of an electric blender and blend until thoroughly mixed, or beat the mixture with a heavy potato masher, making sure you do a thorough job of mixing. Add the sour cream and mix well with a spoon.

Makes about 2½ cups dunk.

Anchovy Dunk

1 can (1¾ ounces) flat anchovy fillets, coarsely chopped
2 cloves garlic, finely chopped
¼ cup pickled cocktail onions, chopped
1 package (4 ounces) cream cheese
Heavy cream or dairy sour cream

Combine the anchovies, garlic, and onions. Mash the cream cheese with a fork, thinning it to the desired consistency with the heavy cream or sour cream. Add to the anchovy mixture, combining all ingredients.

Makes about ¾ cup dunk.

Herbed Sour Cream Dunk
This dunk also makes an excellent dressing for a salad of thin cucumber slices.

2 cups dairy sour cream
¼ cup finely chopped fresh dill
¼ cup finely chopped onion
½ cup chopped parsley
Salt to taste
Dash of lemon juice

Combine the sour cream with the dill, onion, parsley, and salt. Add a dash of lemon juice and let the dunk stand for 1 hour before serving.

Makes about 2¼ cups dunk.

Mustard-Anchovy Dunk

½ cup mayonnaise
½ cup dairy sour cream
¼ cup prepared mustard
2 cloves garlic, finely chopped
1 teaspoon tarragon
2 tablespoons finely chopped parsley
2 tablespoons finely chopped anchovies
Freshly ground pepper to taste

Combine the mayonnaise and sour cream. Add the mustard, garlic, tarragon, parsley, and anchovies, mixing well. Then add pepper.

Makes about 1¼ cups dunk.

CHEESE

A big platter of a variety of good cheeses and a plate of French bread, good, thin-sliced rye or pumpernickel, and crackers, along with some butter for those who like it, is always welcome fare with outdoor drinks.

Cheese Spreads

If you have bits of cheese left in your refrigerator, you can mash them with cream cheese, flavor with a little mustard, and blend well. This makes a first-class spread which can be used for the appetizer tray with crackers or toast or all kinds of vegetables. Here are some good combinations, any of which can be stored in jars in the refrigerator.

Roquefort or Blue Cheese Spread

Blend together leftovers of Roquefort or Danish Blue cheese with cream cheese and butter and flavor with a little Worcestershire sauce and pepper. Mash the cheeses together well and taste for seasoning.

Mustard-Cheddar Spread

Use aged natural cheese, not processed, for spreads.

1 pound sharp Cheddar cheese or country store cheese, grated	2 teaspoons dry mustard
	1 tablespoon Worcestershire sauce
1 package (4 ounces) cream cheese	1 tablespoon chili sauce

Mash the Cheddar cheese into the cream cheese and flavor it with the remaining ingredients. Mix thoroughly, adding more chili sauce if necessary.

Makes about 4 cups spread.

Spicy Pimento-Cheddar Spread

1 pound sharp Cheddar cheese, grated	2 small hot peppers, finely chopped
1 package (8 ounces) cream cheese	1 teaspoon dry mustard Heavy cream or melted butter
1 jar (4 ounces) pimentos, finely chopped	

Mash the Cheddar with the cream cheese and combine them with the pimentos, peppers, and mustard. Add enough cream to make a good paste. Mix well with a fork.

Makes about 5 cups spread.

Garden Cream Cheese Spread

2 packages (8 ounces each) cream cheese	½ cup chopped parsley
1 bunch green onions (2 inches green included), finely sliced	½ cup finely sliced celery Heavy cream or dairy sour cream
6 to 8 radishes, finely sliced	Salt and freshly ground pepper to taste

Soften the cream cheese and blend it with the green onions, radishes, parsley, and celery. Blend well with enough heavy cream to make the mixture easily spreadable. Add salt and pepper. Chill.

To serve: This spread should be cold and goes well with rye bread.

Makes about 3 cups spread.

Sardine-Cream Cheese Spread

1 large can French or Portuguese sardines	1 teaspoon finely chopped onion
1 package (8 ounces) cream cheese Juice of 1 lemon	Salt to taste
	1 teaspoon finely chopped parsley

Thoroughly mash the sardines and combine with the cream cheese, lemon juice, and onion. Beat well with a fork until nicely blended. Taste and add salt if needed and the chopped parsley. Mix again.

Makes about 1 cup spread.

SEAFOOD SNACKS

There is nothing better than smoked or cured fish. I like the freshwater fish—whitefish, carp, buffalo fish, or chub—smoked or kippered. Serve them with lemon wedges and thin slices of salty rye or pumpernickel well buttered. Salmon, sturgeon, and eel, also widely available, make perfect appetizers, too. So does herring, in all forms—marinated, in wine sauce, in sour cream, or smoked. Other delicious snacks include:

Sardines, French or Portuguese in olive oil, skinless and boneless in olive oil, spiced sardines, Norwegian sardines in olive oil, Maine sardines in soybean oil, California sardines in tomato or mustard sauce.

Fine tuna in olive oil is a wonderful snack on crackers or bread with lemon juice. Or it may be mixed with onion, chopped olives, and mayonnaise for a spread.

Mussels, spiced and smoked, and smoked oysters from the Pacific coast make wonderful snacks or appetizers.

SAUSAGE AND PATE

Serve a big platter of several varieties of good sausage, thinly sliced, with thinly sliced buttered pumpernickel or rye bread—and dill pickles.

Here are suggestions for the sausage platter: Salami, summer sausage, thuringer, metwurst, bologna, braunschweiger, cervelat, blood sausage, tongue sausage, mortadella, Lebanon bologna.

Serve a variety of mustards, too. You can make the hot English type by moistening dry mustard with a little white wine; you might also try some French Dijon mustard and some German or Dutch mustards.

Another good sausage appetizer is made by slicing cervelat very thin, combining it with greens and finely cut celery, and dressing it with French dressing or mayonnaise. Add slices of tomato if you like.

Liverwurst Pâté

The result tastes like a pâté that would cost about four times as much. Use the best-quality liverwurst you can find.

1 pound liverwurst	¼ cup heavy cream or
¼ cup finely chopped	dairy sour cream
onion	¼ cup whiskey or cognac
1 teaspoon prepared	
mustard	

Mix all ingredients thoroughly with an electric beater or a fork. Cover and store in the refrigerator.

Makes about 2½ cups pâté.

Country Pâté

1½ pounds pork liver, ground	1 teaspoon salt
1½ pounds pork, ground	1 teaspoon freshly ground pepper
1 large onion, grated	4 eggs, lightly beaten
1 clove garlic, finely chopped	½ pound bacon (approximately)
½ cup chopped parsley	½ cup cognac or whiskey

Preheat oven to 350°F. Combine the ground liver and pork with the onion and garlic. Add to this the parsley, salt, pepper, and eggs. Line a 9x5x3-inch loaf pan with strips of bacon and pour the mixture in. Pour over this the cognac and cover with strips of bacon. Cover with aluminum foil and bake for 1½ to 2 hours or until the pâté has shrunk slightly from the sides of the pan.

Remove from the oven and weight the foil-covered pâté down with some heavy object while it cools. Chill.

To serve: Slice thin and accompany with drinks.

Serves 12 to 14.

Steak Tartare

There is nothing better with drinks than a bowl of freshly ground raw beef—round or sirloin—and plenty of pumpernickel or crackers on which to spread it.

2	pounds round or sirloin, freshly ground	1	teaspoon freshly ground pepper
½	cup finely chopped onion	2	tablespoons A-1 sauce or Worcestershire sauce
2	cloves garlic, chopped		
1	teaspoon salt	¼	cup chopped parsley

Combine all ingredients and mix lightly. Taste for seasoning and add more salt and A-1 or Worcestershire if necessary.

To serve: Mound the tartare in a bowl or shape into individual patties and accompany with bread, crackers, butter, and lots of mustard.

Serves 8 to 12.

POTATOES, RICE, & VEGETABLES

If you are entertaining at home, it is usually easier to prepare any vegetables you are serving to round out the meal in the kitchen or in an electric skillet. However, if you are roughing it or just on a picnic a little more elaborate than usual, many of the recipes in this section can be cooked on an extra outdoor grill. They are marked with an asterisk (*).

POTATOES

*Boiled Potatoes

My favorites are the tiny new potatoes. I cut a thin strip of the skin off around the center of each potato. This keeps the jackets from splitting and curling. I boil them quickly or steam them in plenty of butter in a covered skillet. They are always good.

*Sautéed Potatoes

Potatoes cooked this way with bits of crisp suet are unbelievably good and just the thing with hearty outdoor roasts or steaks.

Slice peeled raw potatoes fairly thin and soak them in cold water for an hour or so. If you are cooking steak or roast beef, cut away some of the beef fat or get a little extra from the butcher. Cut the fat very fine, put it in a skillet (a heavy iron or cast-aluminum skillet is best), and let it melt. You will need about 1 tablespoon of suet per potato. When it is melted and the bits of suet have turned crisp, add the potato slices, after drying them on paper towels, and let them sauté gently. Turn them often with a large spatula. They should be nicely browned, crisp, and cooked through. Don't break them when turning. Add salt and plenty of freshly ground pepper.

French Fried Potatoes

French fries can be soggy and unappetizing or crisp and delicious—depending on how you cook them. I have a theory that frying the potatoes twice gives a crisper product. I cut my potatoes in fairly thin strips and soak them in ice water for an hour or so. I heat the fat to 350°F. in a deep-fat fryer. The electric fryers have thermostats, but with the others you will need a thermometer. I dry the potatoes thoroughly on a towel and fry them in the fat until they are just faintly colored. Then I drain them well and put them on paper towels to cool. This can be done ahead of time—early in the day.

When I am ready to serve the meat courses, I heat the fat again—this time to 370°F.—and plunge the potatoes in, a few at a time. When they are brown and crisp I serve them up piping hot. I would rather have them overcooked than undercooked. At any rate, cooking twice assures you of crisp brown French fries.

Variation

For julienne or shoestring potatoes, cut the potatoes in very small matchlike strips. Fry them at 350°F. until they are really crisp.

Potato Chips

Potato chips are easy to make. Just invest in a wood cutter with diagonal blades, which you can find in a hardware shop. Take good size potatoes, cut them very thin, and soak them in cold water for an hour or two. Dry them thoroughly on a towel. Fry them at 360°F. until they are lightly browned and curled. Don't fry too many at a time or they may stick together. Drain on absorbent paper and salt well.

*Home Fried Potatoes

Start with boiled potatoes in their jackets. Peel and slice medium thin. Sauté slowly in butter or beef fat until slices are browned and crisp around the edges. Turn them as they cook with a spatula, being careful not to break the slices. Salt and pepper to taste.

*Hashed Brown Potatoes

Cut boiled potatoes into small cubes and sauté them in butter or beef fat. Press them down gently in the pan with a spatula or turner so that they will become crusty on the bottom and well browned. Turn them out on a plate or platter, keeping the brown crust on top. Be careful when you do it, or they will simply tumble into a heap. Tilt the pan gently and loosen them with the spatula. Then with a quick flip get them over and out. Season to taste just before dishing up.

*Lyonnaise Potatoes

2 medium onions, chopped
4 tablespoons butter or beef fat
4 or 5 good size boiled potatoes, peeled and sliced

¼ cup chopped parsley
Salt and freshly ground pepper to taste

Sauté the onions in the butter until they are just soft. Add the potatoes and mix them with the onions. Cook slowly until the mixture is browned. Add the parsley and season to taste.

Serves 4.

*Potatoes Hashed in Cream
This is a delicious, rich-tasting way to cook potatoes.

Cut boiled potatoes into cubes and sauté them in butter or beef fat until they are heated through and lightly browned. Sprinkle with a little flour, salt, and freshly ground pepper. Gradually pour in enough heavy cream to cover the bottom of the pan and let the potatoes cook in the cream. Be careful not to let them scorch. Sprinkle liberally with paprika.

*Baked Potatoes
It's easiest to bake the potatoes in the house and bring them out to eat with your grilled meat. I like to split them after baking, add butter, salt, freshly ground pepper, and paprika, and blend it all together. Then I return them to the oven to heat through again.

You can bake potatoes successfully on the top of the grill in a tightly covered cast-aluminum pan. It's a tricky job, but it can be done. You can also bake them in the coals of a dying fire, wrapped in foil.

RICE

Rice and Mushrooms

Cook 1½ cups of rice. Combine with 1 cup of finely chopped mushrooms which have been sautéed in ¼ pound of butter and seasoned well with salt, freshly ground pepper, and a dash of Worcestershire sauce.

Serves 6.

Risi Pisi

Cook 1½ cups of your favorite rice in your favorite marinade. Drain and combine with 2 tins (8½ ounces each) of tiny French peas, which have been heated in their own juice, drained, and combined with ¼ pound or more of melted butter. Toss them well together, sprinkle with a little finely chopped parsley and salt and pepper to taste.

Serves 6.

Herbed Rice

Cook 1½ cups of rice. Combine with ½ cup of finely chopped parsley, ¼ cup of finely chopped chives, and 5 tablespoons of melted butter. Salt and pepper to taste.

Serves 6.

Rice with Green Onions

Cook 1½ cups of rice. Combine with 1 cup of finely chopped green onions which have been sautéed with ¼ pound of butter. Salt and pepper to taste. Sprinkle with chopped parsley.

Serves 6.

Saffron Rice

Cook 1½ cups of rice with a small pinch of saffron and use beef broth or consommé instead of water. Combine the cooked rice with ¼ pound of melted butter and ⅓ cup of grated Romano or Parmesan cheese. Toss lightly and sprinkle lavishly with chopped parsley.

Serves 6.

Rice in Cheese Sauce

Combine 3 cups of cooked rice—this is the equivalent of 1½ cups of uncooked rice—with 1 cup of grated (imported) Swiss cheese and 1 cup of dairy sour cream. Toss the ingredients together over low heat until the cheese is melted and the cream is heated through, but do not allow them to come to a boil. Salt and pepper to taste.

Serves 6.

VEGETABLES

Boiled Corn

There is nothing better in the summer than freshly gathered, tender corn. Don't overcook it. Five minutes in boiling water is ample.

*Grilled Corn

Broiled corn is excellent. Turn the husks back without tearing them off the cob, remove the long silk, dip the corn in cold water, and replace the husks. Place them on the grill and let the ears roast, turning them often. Serve with plenty of butter and salt and pepper.

*Sautéed Corn

2 cloves garlic, finely chopped	⅓ cup heavy cream
¼ cup olive oil	Freshly grated Parmesan cheese or Romano cheese
2 cans (16 ounces each) whole-kernel corn	

Sauté the garlic gently in the olive oil. Add the corn and toss well until it is thoroughly heated. Add the cream and sprinkle lavishly with the cheese. Allow the dish to simmer for 3 to 4 minutes before serving.

Serves 4.

French Fried Eggplant

Peel the eggplant and slice it rather thin. Soak the slices in ice water for an hour or so. Dry them, dip in flour, and fry in deep fat heated to 360°F. until crisp and nicely browned. Drain and season to taste.

*Grilled Eggplant Slices

This versatile vegetable is especially good with barbecued meats.

Peel the eggplant and cut in slices ¾ of an inch thick. Dredge them lightly with flour, dot with butter, and brush with oil. Broil over charcoal as you would a hamburger, turning once during the cooking. Brush again with oil after you turn them and season to taste.

Variation

Sprinkle each slice with grated cheese just as you turn it.

French Fried Onions

Slice onions fairly thin and separate into rings. Soak in milk for 30 minutes and drain on absorbent paper. Sprinkle with flour and fry, a few rings at a time, in fat heated to 365°F. I like them well done—but take them out when they are cooked to your taste. Drain and salt.

*Grilled Onions

Great slices of Bermuda onions can be put in a folding grill, brushed with butter, and broiled until they are a golden brown. They are best if a little underdone in the center and still crunchy. They can also be prepared in the same fashion under the broiler of your kitchen range.

*Smothered Onions

You can fix these on your grill if you have a heavy skillet and enough room for it. Peel and cut the onions in rather thick slices. Melt 4 to 5 tablespoons of butter in a heavy skillet, add the onion slices, and cover the pan tightly. Cook very slowly until the onions are tender but not browned. Sprinkle with salt to taste and add a goodly coating of grated Swiss or American cheese. Cover again until the cheese melts.

*Grilled Tomatoes

In selecting tomatoes for cooking be sure they are not overripe or too juicy. Cut them in halves, flour them lightly, or dip in crumbs, and broil over a low fire.

*Sautéed Tomatoes

This is really a more successful method than broiling is.

Halve the tomatoes and sauté them in a skillet with a little butter or oil until they are just cooked through. A sprinkling of basil, either fresh or dried, or of basil seasoning powder does wonders.

*Pennsylvania Dutch Tomatoes

This makes a delicious breakfast or brunch dish for Sunday morning.

You will need firm tomatoes, either ripe or green, for this dish. Cut them in thick slices and dip them in flour. Sauté in butter or bacon fat and before turning sprinkle the top side with brown sugar. Then turn and let the sugar melt into the fat and brown. Sprinkle with a little more sugar and let it melt down on top. Just before serving, cover only to the top of the tomato slices with heavy cream. Let it come to a boil and thicken.

To serve: These are excellent dished up on toast and accompanied with fried bacon strips.

*Tomatoes Sicilion

These are made in a covered skillet and cooked gently for quite a while.

4 to 6 tomatoes	3 cloves garlic, chopped
Olive oil	Salt and freshly ground
¼ cup chopped parsley	pepper to taste
¼ cup chopped fresh basil	Cinnamon

Cut off the stem ends of the tomatoes and discard. Cover the bottom of a skillet with olive oil. Add the parsley, basil, and garlic, and season with salt and pepper. Place the tomatoes, cut-side-down, on this bed of seasonings. Sprinkle them with just a trace of cinnamon. Cover the pan and cook very slowly until the tomatoes are just heated through.

To serve: These tomatoes are excellent with pork or lamb.

Serves 4 to 6.

French Fried Zucchini

The small green Italian squash called "zucchini" makes an excellent outdoor vegetable. It cooks quickly and goes well with many foods.

Cut unpeeled zucchini in very thin slices and dredge them lightly in flour. Fry them in fat heated to 365°F. until they are crisp and cooked through—about 5 minutes. Drain and season.

*Sautéed Zucchini

This dish can be prepared quickly on top of the grill. Cut 6 small zucchini in quarters without peeling them. Heat 5 tablespoons of olive oil in an iron skillet. Add the zucchini and 2 cloves of shredded garlic. Sauté lightly for 5 to 8 minutes, turning frequently with a spatula. Cover the pan and cook for 2 or 3 minutes more. Season to taste.

Serves 4 to 6.

CASSEROLES

Some of the food you eat out of doors will have to be cooked indoors, which means that kitchen duty will have to be done. If you are planning a beach or picnic barbecue that will take you far from home, however, do not feel that you must rule these tasty side dishes off your menu. Insulated bags and boxes will bring your kitchen-made casseroles piping hot to the barbecue site.

Baked Eggplant Casserole

1 large or 2 medium eggplants, cut in ½-inch slices	3 green peppers, seeded and sliced
Seasoned flour	Butter
⅓ cup olive oil	Grated Parmesan cheese
3 large onions, sliced	Salt and freshly ground pepper to taste
6 ripe tomatoes, peeled and sliced	Bread crumbs

Dip the eggplant slices in the seasoned flour and sauté in olive oil until lightly browned. Reserve the oil. In a good-sized casserole, alternate layers of eggplant with onions, tomatoes, and peppers, dotting each layer with butter and sprinkling with Parmesan and salt and pepper. Make the top layer eggplant and over it pour the reserved olive oil, adding more if the mixture seems dry. Sprinkle with bread crumbs and more Parmesan. Cover and bake in a preheated oven at 375°F. for about 45 minutes, or until the casserole is bubbling and the top brown.

Serves 6 to 8.

String Bean and Mushroom Casserole

1½ pounds string beans, split lengthwise	½ pound mushrooms, sliced
¼ pound butter	Grated Parmesan cheese

Cook beans in a small amount of boiling salted water until they are just tender. Drain and set aside. Reserve a tablespoon or two of the butter and melt the remainder. Sauté the mushrooms until just heated through. Add the beans and cook together very quickly, stirring constantly. Remove to a casserole, sprinkle with grated Parmesan, and dot with the reserved butter. Bake covered in a preheated oven at 350°F. for 15 minutes, or until the cheese is melted and browned.

Serves 6.

Lima Bean Casserole

2 cloves garlic, finely chopped	1 teaspoon freshly ground pepper
6 to 8 green onions, finely chopped	1 can (4 ounces) tomato sauce
¼ cup olive oil	2 packages (10 ounces each) frozen lima beans, cooked
4 medium tomatoes, peeled, seeded, and finely chopped	Grated Romano or Parmesan cheese
1 teaspoon basil	Butter
1 teaspoon salt	

In a skillet, sauté the garlic and green onions in the olive oil until soft but not browned. Add the tomatoes, basil, salt, and pepper and cook slowly for 20 minutes. Add the tomato sauce, bring the mixture to a boil, and cook for 5 minutes. Pour this sauce over the lima beans and blend well. Pour the mixture into an oiled casserole. Sprinkle with grated cheese and dot with butter. Bake covered in a preheated oven at 350°F. for 20 to

25 minutes, or until the cheese is melted and the beans heated through.

Serves 6.

Summer Vegetable Casserole

1 cup cooked French-style string beans
1 cup cooked green peas (fresh, frozen, or canned)
1 cup cooked whole-kernel corn (fresh, frozen, or canned)
1 cup cooked tiny onions (fresh, frozen, or canned)
4 tablespoons butter
3 tablespoons flour

1 cup heavy cream
½ cup grated Cheddar cheese or imported Swiss cheese
Salt and freshly ground pepper to taste
1 teaspoon dry mustard
Dash of Worcestershire sauce
Grated Parmesan cheese

Combine the cooked vegetables in an ovenproof casserole. Melt the butter in a saucepan and stir in the flour. Cook together until well blended. Gradually stir in the cream and continue stirring until the sauce is well thickened. Add the grated Cheddar, salt and pepper, mustard, and Worcestershire. Stir until the cheese is melted, then pour over the cooked vegetables. Sprinkle with Parmesan. Cover and bake in a preheated oven at 350°F. until the vegetables are thoroughly reheated and blended with the sauce.

Serves 6 to 8.

Corn Casserole

¼ cup finely chopped green onion
¼ cup finely chopped green pepper
¼ cup olive oil
2 cans (8 ounces each) whole-kernel corn

½ cup grated imported Swiss cheese
½ cup heavy cream
Butter
Sesame seeds

Sauté the green onion and green pepper in the olive oil for 5 minutes. Place them in a buttered 2-quart casserole and blend in the corn, grated Swiss cheese, and heavy cream. Dot with butter, sprinkle with sesame seeds, cover, and bake in a preheated oven 350°F. for 20 to 25 minutes.

Serves 4 to 6.

Onion Casserole
Canned bouillon or consommé works perfectly for this recipe.

6 medium to large size onions	½ cup coarsely grated Cheddar or imported Swiss cheese
1 can (10½ ounces) beef bouillon or consommé	

Cut the onions into rather thick slices. Place them in a well-buttered 2-quart casserole and add the bouillon. Cover and bake in a preheated oven at 350°F. for approximately 20 minutes. Add the grated cheese and return uncovered to the oven for 5 to 7 minutes before serving.

Serves 4 to 6.

Ratatouille
The quantities in this recipe may be increased and the dish is equally delicious when served cold with additional oil to which a dash of orange or lemon juice has been added. In this case it is pleasant to combine the dish with black olives and sautéed mushrooms.

⅓ cup olive oil	3 tomatoes, peeled and sliced
3 medium size zucchini, sliced but not peeled	Salt and freshly ground pepper to taste
1 eggplant, diced	Pinch of basil or oregano
1 large onion, finely chopped	
1 clove garlic, finely chopped	

185

Heat the olive oil in a large skillet. Sauté the zucchini slices and the eggplant in the oil until tender and nicely browned. Add the onion and garlic and continue cooking until soft and well blended with the eggplant and zucchini. Lastly add the tomatoes and let it all cook over a brisk heat for 10 to 15 minutes or until it is well mixed and has the appearance of a vegetable stew—which it is. Salt and pepper (adding a pinch of basil or oregano) and transfer to an oval or round baking dish which may be used for serving.

Serves 4 to 6.

Mushroom-Barley Casserole

1 large onion	1 cup pearl barley
½ pound mushrooms	2 cups meat or
4 to 5 tablespoons butter	chicken broth

Peel and chop the onion. Wipe the mushrooms with a damp cloth and slice them. Melt the butter and sauté the onion and mushrooms until soft. Add the barley and lightly brown it. Pour this mixture into a buttered casserole. Be sure to taste the broth for seasoning before you pour it over the barley; add salt and pepper if needed. Pour 1 cup of liquid over the barley in the casserole and cover. Bake in a 350°F. over for ½ hour and then uncover and add the second cup of broth. Continue baking until the liquid is absorbed and the barley is done. In place of chicken or meat broth, you may also make your own broth, using 3 bouillon cubes to 2 cups boiling water.

Variations

● While you are baking the barley, take an additional ½ pound whole mushrooms and sauté them in butter. Let them cook down until they are very rich, almost black. Mix with plenty of whole toasted almonds and spread this mixture over the top just before serving.

This dish goes particularly well with poultry and game, I find.

● Cook 1 pound of gizzards until tender in water, salt and pepper, and an herb of your choice. Use the broth to finish the casserole after the preliminary steps. Slice the gizzards and mix into the barley.

SALADS &
SALAD DRESSING

SALADS

Raw Vegetable Bowl

Either for an appetizer or a side dish, I like raw vegetables with plain salt and pepper or with a dunking sauce. I like to use endive, celery, cucumber, onions, and pickles. They should all be thoroughly iced and crisp. Salt and pepper is really all you need, but if you want a dressing, make it a separate bowl of highly seasoned mayonnaise into which the greens can be dunked.

To season mayonnaise for this, add chopped garlic, onion, hard-cooked egg, capers, and a touch of tomato.

If you are serving a Sunday breakfast party, try radishes—crisp and cold—with a little butter. This is a French and German idea; you'll have to try it to see how good it is.

Green Salad

Green salad is standard at most outdoor parties. It goes very well with beefsteak or hearty hamburgers. Be sure your greens are crisp and dry. Water dilutes the dressing. Get a salad basket into which you can put the greens to shake off all the water, or dry them by wrapping loosely in a clean towel and shaking.

Break your greens in bite-size pieces into your bowl. Make a dressing of four parts oil to one part wine vinegar or lemon juice. I prefer the latter. Add salt and freshly ground pepper to taste and any seasonings you like, such as mustard, garlic, herbs, Worcestershire sauce, or Angostura bitters. Pour the dressing over the greens and toss at the last minute. Tossing should be done thoroughly. Dig down to the bottom of the bowl with your fork and spoon and bring each piece of green up to the top so that it gets a good coating of dressing.

Variations

● For a Caesar salad, sprinkle a little grated Italian cheese—Parmesan or Romano—into the dressing, add a few chopped anchovies, some croutons (squares of bread cooked in olive oil and garlic until crisp), and a raw egg. Mix this thoroughly and pour over the greens. It's very filling, so don't serve it with a heavy meal.
● Add quartered tomatoes, sliced cucumbers, and sliced radishes to the greens. This is a Chiffonade salad.
● Add cooked green beans and green peas to the greens, toss the salad, and top with thin raw onion rings. This is very good with chicken.
● Add a few chilled shrimp to the salad.
● Add hunks of crabmeat.
● Add bits of crisp bacon for a delicate touch.

Sweet and Sour Cucumber Salad
This simple dish is unbelievably good.

2	large cucumbers, peeled and sliced paper thin		Salt and freshly ground pepper to taste
½	cup red wine vinegar	¼	cup chopped onion (optional)
½	cup water		
1½	tablespoons sugar	¼	cup chopped parsley (optional)
¼	cup salad oil		

189

Put the cucumbers in a serving bowl. Combine the remaining ingredients and pour them over the cucumbers. Let chill for at least an hour or two. In fact, it can be made the day before you use it.

To serve: This salad is perfect with fish or cold meats or as a first course for a late Sunday breakfast.

Serves 4.

Cucumber Salad with Sour Cream Dressing

Peel two good-sized cucumbers and split them in half. With a spoon, scrape out the seeds and throw them away. Slice the cucumber shells very thin. Place them in a bowl and season with salt. Cover with equal parts of mayonnaise and dairy sour cream and chill for 2 to 3 hours.

Serves 4.

Variations

● Add finely chopped fresh dill to the dressing.
● Add chopped chives or green onions to the dressing.
● Add chopped tarragon to the dressing.

Cole Slaw

This hearty salad is ideal for outdoor eating. It can be made well in advance, as it improves with mellowing.

1 large head white or red cabbage, finely shredded	¼ cup salad oil
	3 tablespoon sugar
	¼ cup red wine vinegar
1 cup dairy sour cream, heavy cream, or buttermilk	½ teaspoon celery seeds
	½ teaspoon mustard seeds
	Salt to taste

Wash the shredded cabbage and dry it well. Place it in a large bowl. Blend the remaining ingredients and pour over the salad. Toss well and let the salad stand in a cold place at least an hour or two before serving. Vary

190

the sugar and the cream in the dressing to suit your own taste.

Serves 6.

Tangy Cole Slaw

1	large head white or red cabbage, finely shredded	1	tablespoon sugar
		1	teaspoon dry mustard
1	cup dairy sour cream	1	tablespoon prepared horseradish
	Juice of 1 lemon		Salt to taste

Wash the shredded cabbage and dry it well. Place it in a large bowl. Blend the remaining ingredients and thin down with a little water if necessary. Pour the dressing over the salad and toss it well. Let stand in a cold place at least an hour or two before serving.

Serves 6.

Cole Slaw with Mayonnaise Dressing

1	large head white or red cabbage, finely shredded	1	tablespoon sugar
		½	teaspoon celery seeds
1	cup mayonnaise	½	teaspoon mustard seeds
½	cup dairy sour cream		Salt and freshly ground pepper to taste
	Juice of 1 lemon		

Wash the shredded cabbage and dry it well. Place it in a large bowl. Blend the remaining ingredients and pour them over the salad. Toss well and let stand in a cold place at least an hour or two before serving.

Serves 6.

Onion Salad

Good raw onions, thinly sliced, are classic fare with hearty outdoor meat dishes. The red Italian or Spanish onions are especially good and can be found all summer long. Bermuda onions are fine, too. Just serve them with salt and pepper, or add a little vinegar or oil and vinegar.

Onion and Tomato Salad

Great slabs of raw onion alternated with thick slices of ripe beefsteak tomatoes make a delicious salad with any grilled dish. You can add strips of green pepper and fingers of cucumber if you like. Again, just salt and pepper—or a little vinegar and oil.

Potato Salad

Of the many versions of this famous salad, here is my favorite.

6 to 8 medium potatoes	½ teaspoon celery seeds
1 cup olive oil or peanut oil	½ teaspoon mustard seeds
⅓ cup red wine vinegar	½ cup finely chopped onion
1 teaspoon salt	¼ cup finely chopped parsley
1 teaspoon freshly ground pepper	

Boil the potatoes in their jackets until just barely done. While they are still hot, peel them and slice them into a bowl. You can manage the hot potatoes with a fork and a little cold running water.

Combine the oil, vinegar, salt, and pepper in a small pan and heat. When the mixture reaches the boiling point, pour it over the potato slices. Add the celery seeds and mustard seeds and let the potatoes cool. Cover and chill until you are ready to use.

Before serving, add the onion and parsley. Add more oil and vinegar if necessary. Taste for seasoning.

Serves 6 to 8.

White Bean or Lentil Salad

This is a wonderful dish to serve with Spitted Spareribs (page 98).

1½	cups white beans or lentils	3	tablespoons wine vinegar
1	onion, stuck with 2 cloves		Salt and freshly ground pepper to taste
1	bay leaf		
⅔	cup olive oil or cooking oil	½	cup chopped onion
		¼	cup chopped parsley
			Lettuce leaves
			Chopped parsley

Follow the directions on the package for soaking and cooking the beans, adding to the water in which you cook them the onion stuck with cloves and the bay leaf. Don't let the beans boil, just simmer them. When they are just tender, drain.

Combine the olive oil, vinegar, and salt and pepper and pour this sauce over the beans while they are still hot. Let the beans cool in this mixture and put them in the refrigerator to chill. Just before serving add the chopped onion and ¼ cup chopped parsley. Toss the salad well, arrange it in a bowl lined with lettuce leaves, and top with more chopped parsley.

Serves 6.

SALAD DRESSINGS

Basic French Dressing

The classic French dressing is simply 3 to 4 parts of olive oil to 1 part of wine vinegar or lemon juice, and salt and pepper to taste. It should be mixed just before serving.

Other oils, such as peanut oil or corn oil, may be substituted for the olive oil, but the flavor will not be the same. Be sure your wine vinegar is the real thing. Some on the market are imitations and are much too vinegary. If you like a little additional flavor, such as tarragon or some other herb, I suggest that you add the flavoring yourself to suit your taste instead of buying ready-flavored vinegars.

Do not store your salad oil—whether olive, peanut, or corn oil—in the refrigerator. It will turn cloudy. On the other hand, oil kept in an opened container in warm temperatures will turn rancid. Keep it in a cool spot and during hot summer months buy in small quantities.

Mayonnaise

There are several secrets to making good mayonnaise. First, use only good olive oil and the best fresh eggs. Second, have all ingredients at room temperature. And third, add the oil very slowly.

Select a shallow dish and use a silver fork for mixing. Start with 2 egg yolks, add salt to taste, and a bit of dry mustard. Blend them thoroughly with the fork, and then start adding the olive oil, beating thoroughly all the while. You will need about 1 cup of oil. If it begins to curdle, start another batch with 1 egg yolk and some oil and gradually stir in the curdled mixture. If the dressing seems to be getting too thick, add a few drops of lemon juice or vinegar. Continue adding the oil and beating until all the oil is used up. Taste for seasoning. You may want to add more salt, lemon juice, or vinegar, or perhaps some cayenne.

This makes a rich, thick mayonnaise that is thoroughly delicious.

Makes about 1¼ cups sauce.

Remoulade Sauce

To 1 cup of mayonnaise add 1 teaspoon of dry mustard, 1 tablespoon of anchovies finely chopped, 1 tablespoon of chopped parsley, 1 clove of garlic grated, some capers and chopped hard-cooked egg, a bit of tarragon, and chopped olives if you like. Some people like to add horseradish and chopped green pepper, too.

Makes about 1¼ cups sauce.

Green Mayonnaise

To mayonnaise add finely chopped parsley, spinach, chives, tarragon, and chervil. Flavor with a little grated garlic.

Russian Dressing

To mayonnaise add chili sauce, chopped onion, chopped olives, and chopped hard-cooked egg to taste.

Tuna Mayonnaise

To mayonnaise add 1 small can of tuna mashed, 2 or 3 anchovies mashed, and a dash of lemon juice,

SAUCES & MARINADES

STEAK AND BARBECUE SAUCES

When it comes to sauces, most dyed-in-the-wool barbe-
cuers like to express their own individualities. This is
all to the good, provided you don't mix ingredients
whose flavors conflict. There are certain classical combinations that have stood the test of time, and these
with a bit of variation answer all purposes. Here are
proven recipes for the basic sauces for meats, fish, and
vegetables.

A good thing to keep in mind when cooking any
sauce is that if it seems too thin at the end of the given
cooking period, you can always reduce it and thicken it
by cooking it over high heat, with the cover off, until it
reaches the desired consistency.

For dishes that should be marinated a long time—
such as shish kebab—put the cubes of meat in a jar
with a lid. Cover them with the marinade and put the
lid on. Then if you do not use all of the meat, you can
leave it in the jar in the sauce and keep it in the
refrigerator.

Simple Steak Sauce

I'm sure you'll find this blend of flavors unique and satisfying—and it's an easy sauce to make.

¼	pound butter	1	cup white wine
1½	cups chopped shallots, green onions, or scallions	¼	cup chopped parsley
		2	tablespoons butter
1	teaspoon salt		Freshly ground pepper to taste

Melt the ¼ pound of butter in a skillet and add the shallots. Do not brown them—merely let them blend together and wilt down. Add the salt and wine and bring to a boil. Lower the heat and simmer for 5 minutes. Add the parsley and 2 tablespoons of butter. Boil for 3 minutes, add some pepper, and taste for seasoning.

To serve: This sauce goes well with any broiled or roasted meat as well as with steak.

Makes about 1¾ cups sauce.

Anchovy Steak Sauce

Add 3 tablespoons of finely chopped anchovies to Simple Steak Sauce (opposite) just before removing from the heat. Blend thoroughly.

Tarragon Steak Sauce

Following the recipe for Simple Steak Sauce (above), use 2 cups of chopped shallots or green onions. Add 1 tablespoon of fresh or 1½ teaspoons of dried tarragon. Substitute red wine for the white and add a dash of vinegar.

Devil Sauce

5 or 6 tablespoons butter
3 cloves garlic, finely chopped
1 medium onion, finely chopped
¼ cup chopped pickle
2 tablespoons vinegar
½ cup catsup
½ cup Worcestershire sauce
1 teaspoon salt
1 teaspoon dry mustard
Dash or two of Tabasco sauce
Capers

Heat the butter in a skillet and sauté the garlic and onion until they are just soft. Add the pickle, vinegar, catsup, and Worcestershire. Bring to a boil and add the salt, mustard, Tabasco, and a few capers.

If you like a thicker sauce, add small balls of flour and butter kneaded together and stir until the sauce is thickened and smooth.

To serve: This sauce goes with any meat or poultry dish calling for a deviled sauce or a pungent sauce.

Makes about 2 cups sauce.

Creole Steak Sauce

½ pound butter
1 cup catsup
½ cup Worcestershire sauce
1 onion stuck with 3 cloves
2 cloves garlic
1 cup consommé
1 tablespoon prepared mustard
1 teaspoon salt
½ teaspoon freshly ground pepper

Mix all ingredients in a skillet, bring to a boil, and simmer for 30 minutes. Remove it from the heat and put the sauce through a food mill or mix it in an electric blender. Return the sauce to the skillet and simmer it again for 10 minutes.

This sauce will keep in the refrigerator or it may be frozen for longer storage.

Makes about 3 cups sauce.

Basic Barbecue Sauce

Here is a basic sauce that you can vary in as many ways as your imagination and taste suggest.

5 to 7 cloves garlic, chopped	½ cup brown sugar or honey
2 teaspoons coarse salt	1 teaspoon rosemary or rosemary seasoning powder
2 onions, finely chopped	
1 cup olive oil or peanut oil	½ teaspoon thyme
1 cup tomato sauce or strained canned tomatoes	3 tablespoons chopped green onions
	¼ cup chopped parsley
1 cup Worcestershire sauce	
1 cup red wine vinegar	

Press the garlic into the salt and add the onions. Heat the oil in a skillet, add the garlic and onion mixture, and let it wilt down and blend thoroughly. When the garlic and onions are soft, add the remaining ingredients. Bring to a boil, lower the heat, and simmer for 20 minutes. Taste for seasoning. You may strain it if you wish, or put it in the container of an electric blender to get a smoother mixture.

To serve: Use this sauce hot or cold with either meat or fish. Baste with it and serve with the finished dish.

Makes about 4½ cups sauce.

Variations

Mexican: Add 3 tablespons chili powder and a few finely chopped hot chilies to the sauce before cooking. Add a few dashes of Tabasco sauce if you like it extra hot.

199

Italian: Omit the Worcestershire sauce and the vinegar. Add 1 cup tomato puree, 1 tablespoon of fresh basil or 1 teaspoon dried basil, a pinch of oregano, and 1 cup of red wine. You may add 1 cup of consommé if you wish.

Californian: Omit the vinegar and sugar. Add 1 cup of red wine, the grated rind of 1 orange, ½ cup of orange juice, the juice of 1 lemon, and 1 cup of finely chopped ripe olives.

Tabasco Barbecue Sauce

1 cup vinegar	½ teaspoon Tabasco sauce
1 clove garlic, crushed	1 tablespoon sugar
2 tablespoons Worcestershire sauce	½ cup catsup
1 teaspoon dry mustard	1 teaspoon salt

Combine all ingredients and simmer 10 minutes.

To use and serve: Brush chicken, spareribs, or other meats with this sauce before broiling, baste with it during cooking, and serve as a sauce with the finished dish.

Makes about 1½ cups sauce.

Uncooked Barbecue Sauce
Nothing could be simpler than this sauce.

2 cloves garlic, crushed	1 teaspoon dry mustard
1½ teaspoons salt	Juice of 1 lemon
1 teaspoon freshly ground pepper or crushed pepper	⅓ cup A-1 sauce or steak sauce
¼ cup finely sliced scallions or green onions	2 cups tomato sauce, tomato puree or strained canned tomatoes
2 teaspoons prepared mustard	Dash of Tabasco sauce (optional)

Combine all ingredients and shake furiously in a cocktail shaker or blend in the container of an electric blender. Taste for seasoning. If it seems a little too sharp, add a touch of brown sugar.

Makes about 2¾ cups sauce.

Pungent Barbecue Sauce

1	cup peanut oil or olive oil	1	tablespoon basil
6	cloves garlic, chopped	1	tablespoon chili powder
1	cup finely chopped onion or shallots	¼	cup chopped parsley
1	cup finely chopped green pepper	1	cup red wine
1	cup peeled and finely chopped tomatoes	1	cup consommé or bouillon
1	or 2 stalks celery, finely chopped	1	tablespoon vinegar
		1	cup tomato puree
		1½	teaspoons salt
		1	teaspoon freshly ground pepper

Heat the oil in a large skillet and sauté the garlic until browned and almost crisp. Add the onion and cook until just wilted and soft but not brown. Add the green pepper, tomatoes, celery, basil, chili powder, and parsley. Pour over this the wine, consommé, and vinegar. Cover and simmer for about 40 minutes.

Put the sauce through a strainer or blend it in the container of an electric blender. Add the remaining ingredients and simmer again for 10 minutes. The longer this sauce simmers the better it is.

To serve: It may be used either hot or cold for basting or serving with meats or fish.

Makes about 5½ cups sauce.

California Barbecue Sauce

For an excellent barbecue sauce for beef or pork, use the following ingredients:

201

1	onion, finely chopped	¼	cup brown sugar
1	clove garlic, minced	¼	cup vinegar
1	teaspoon salt	1	can (16 ounces)
⅛	teaspoon freshly		tomato sauce
	ground pepper	1	can (4 ounces)
½	teaspoon chili powder		tomato puree
½	teaspoon celery salt	1	slice lemon
½	teaspoon dry mustard	⅛	teaspoon Tabasco
1	tablespoon		sauce
	Worcestershire sauce		

Combine ingredients in your skillet or saucepan in order listed, over medium heat. Cover and simmer for about 20 minutes, or until sauce reaches desired consistency.

Makes about 3½ cups sauce.

Salsa Fria

This is a famous Mexican sauce which I find can be used for many barbecue dishes. It's simple to make and can easily be added to. Use the canned tomatoes if you can't get good fresh home-grown tomatoes.

2	to 2½ pounds, ripe tomatoes, peeled, seeded, and chopped, or 1 can (28 ounces) solid-pack tomatoes, chopped Fresh or dried hot peppers, chopped	1	teaspoon freshly ground or cracked pepper
		1	large onion, finely chopped
		1	clove garlic, chopped
		2	tablespoons lemon juice or vinegar
1	teaspoon salt	¼	cup olive oil

Blend all ingredients well and chill. Follow your taste about the amount hot peppers used.

To serve: Accompany grilled food or almost any meat or fish dish with this sauce.

Makes about 4 cups sauce.

Variations

● Add finely chopped green pepper.
● Substitute canned Italian plum tomatoes for the solid-pack tomatoes.
● Add finely chopped cucumbers.

Mexican Barbecue Sauce I

6	tablespoons bacon fat or margarine	2	tablespoon chili powder
3	large onions, finely chopped	1	teaspoon cumin
2	cloves garlic, finely chopped	1	bay leaf, crumbled
1	pound ground beef		Consommé or water
			Salt to taste
			Dash of Tabasco sauce (optional)

Melt the bacon fat in a skillet and add the onions and garlic. Sauté until just soft. Add the ground beef and mix well. Sauté for 4 or 5 minutes. Add the chili powder, cumin, and bay leaf and cover with consommé. Simmer the mixture until well blended and thickened. Salt to taste and add a dash of Tabasco if you like.

Combine all ingredients and blend well.

To serve: This goes well over frankfurters or hamburgers with finely chopped raw onions and ripe olives. It is also a superb sauce for rice or spaghetti.

Makes about 3 cups sauce.

Mexican Barbecue Sauce II

This sauce is useful for many different dishes and is especially good for barbecuing turkey or chicken. It is better made the day before so that it will mellow overnight.

6	to 8 mild chili peppers	2	cups chicken broth
2	or 3 hot chili peppers	1	can (4 ounces) green molé sauce
2	or 3 pimentos, finely chopped	1	can (4 ounces) tomato puree (optional)
6	tablespoons bacon fat or lard	½	cup red or white wine (optional)
3	large onions, finely chopped	¼	cup chopped almonds (optional)

Soak the chili peppers in water for several hours. Remove the seeds. Force the mild chilies through the food mill. Chop the hot chilies very fine and combine with the mild chilies and pimentos.

Melt the bacon fat in a skillet and sauté the onions until they are just soft. Add the pepper mixture, chicken broth, molé, and, if desired, the tomato puree and wine. Cook the mixture down for 1 or 2 hours. Correct the seasoning and add the chopped almonds.

To serve: If the sauce accompanies a barbecued turkey, have this wonderful Mexican bean dish with it: Cook up some black or kidney beans. Then toss them in a skillet with plenty of fat or butter, season them with garlic, and mash them down to a paste. Put a large glob of dairy sour cream on each portion.

Makes about 4 cups sauce.

Chinese Barbecue Sauce

This simple sauce is powerful and pungent—the best for marinating and basting Chinese barbecue dishes.

1	cup soy sauce	1	tablespoon grated fresh gingerroot or chopped dried gingerroot
1	teaspoon monosodium glutamate		
2	or 3 cloves garlic, finely chopped	½	cup sherry

Combine all ingredients and blend well.

Makes about 1½ cups sauce.

SERVING SAUCES

Chinese Sweet and Sour Sauce

½	cup wine vinegar	1	large green pepper, cut in strips
½	cup water	3	large tomatoes, cut in wedges
1	cup sugar		
2	tablespoons soy sauce	1½	tablespoons cornstarch
½	cup white wine or sherry	2	tablespoons vinegar
1	cup pineapple chunks	2	tablespoons water
3	or 4 green onions, cut in strips		

Combine in a skillet the ½ cup vinegar, ½ cup water, sugar, soy sauce, white wine, pineapple chunks, green onions, green pepper, and tomatoes. Bring to a boil. Mix the cornstarch with the 2 tablespoons vinegar and 2 tablespoons water. Stir slowly into the sauce until it thickens. Taste for seasoning.

To serve: This is an excellent sauce with any dish calling for a sweet-sour sauce.

Makes about 4 to 5 cups sauce.

Creole Sauce

¼	pound butter	1	can (28 ounces) solid-pack tomatoes
1	large onion, coarsely chopped	1½	cups tomato juice
2	cloves garlic, coarsely chopped	1	teaspoon salt
2	green peppers, coarsely chopped	1	teaspoon freshly ground pepper
2	stalks celery, coarsely chopped	1	teaspoon thyme or oregano
½	cup sherry	½	cup brown sugar
		3	tablespoons vinegar

Melt the butter in a large sauce pan and sauté the onion, garlic, green peppers, and celery for 5 minutes. Add the sherry, cover the pan, and simmer for 20 minutes. Add the remaining ingredients and simmer for 30 minutes.

To serve: This sauce is excellent with any Creole-style meat or fish dish.

Makes about 6½ cups sauce.

Variation

Many people like the addition of gumbo filé and a few pieces of whole okra. Canned and frozen okra are generally available; for the Louisiana flavoring, gumbo filé, try the specialty groceries.

Italian Sauce

This delicious sauce for hamburgers or spaghetti is no cinch to make, but the results are well worth the time and effort.

½ cup olive oil	4 tablespoons olive oil or beef fat
1 can (33 ounces) small Italian plum tomatoes or 2 pounds ripe plum tomatoes, split in two	3 cloves garlic, finely chopped
	½ teaspoon thyme
	½ cup pitted ripe olives, chopped
1 tablespoon fresh basil or 1 teaspoon dried basil	¼ cup finely chopped green pepper
1 teaspoon salt	1 teaspoon salt
1 pound ground beef	1 teaspoon freshly ground pepper
½ pound ground pork	1 cup red wine

Heat the ½ cup olive oil in a large skillet, add the tomatoes, basil, and 1 teaspoon salt and simmer slowly for 1½ hours. Strain through a fine sieve.

While the tomatoes are simmering, sauté the ground beef and pork in the 4 tablespoons of olive oil until the meat loses color. Add the remaining ingredients and simmer for 30 minutes. Combine this with the tomato sauce and let the whole mixture simmer for another 30 minutes. Taste for seasoning.

To serve: Accompany spaghetti, noodles, meats, or poultry with this sauce or use it for basting. When you use it as a sauce for spaghetti or noodles, serve plenty of grated Parmesan or Romano cheese with it.

Makes about 8 cups sauce.

Variations

● If you like your sauce with a stronger tomato flavor, add one 4-ounce can of tomato puree during the last 20 minutes of cooking.

● You can turn this into a delicious chili sauce by adding 2 tablespoons of chili powder or some of the canned prepared chili sauce sold in Mexican stores in a quantity to suit your taste.

● You can make a substitute Chinese curry sauce by adding 4 tablespoons of soy sauce, 3 tablespoons of finely chopped gingerroot, and 1 to 2 tablespoons of curry powder, according to your taste. This is delicious served with barbecued shrimp, barbecued lamb, or beef.

Anchovy Butter Sauce

Melt 6 tablespoons of butter in a small skillet, add 1 or more tablespoons of anchovy paste or crush several anchovy fillets in the butter. Add a few drops of lemon juice.

To serve: This sauce is excellent with fish or steak.

Serves 6.

Tabasco Butter

¼ pound butter or margarine	¼ teaspoon Tabasco sauce
½ teaspoon salt Juice of ½ lemon	1 teaspoon chopped parsley (optional)

Cream the butter until it is fluffy. Stir in the remaining ingredients and chill.

To serve: This goes well with broiled fish.

Makes about ½ cup sauce.

Hollandaise Sauce

Cut ¼ pound of butter into 3 parts. Place one piece in the upper part of a double boiler with 3 egg yolks. Put over hot, but not boiling, water and beat constantly with a wire whisk. As the butter melts, add another piece until all the butter is beaten into the egg yolks. Never let the water boil. Beat until the sauce thickens, add salt to taste, and season with the juice of a lemon or 1 tablespoon of tarragon vinegar. If the sauce curdles, add a little boiling water, a few drops at a time, until the sauce smooths out again.

Makes about 1 cup sauce.

Variation

Add ½ teaspoon of dry mustard to the sauce.

Blender Hollandaise Sauce

In a small saucepan heat ¼ pound butter to bubbling, but do not let it brown. Into the container of the blender put 3 egg yolks, 2 tablespoons of lemon juice, ¼ teaspoon of salt, and a pinch of cayenne. Cover container and flick motor quickly on and off high speed. Remove cover, turn motor on high, and gradually add the hot butter.

To serve: Hollandaise goes well on cooked broccoli, asparagus, cauliflower, or poached eggs.

Makes about ¾ cup sauce.

Béarnaise Sauce

Put 3 shallots or green onions, a sprig of parsley, a sprig of tarragon (or a pinch of dried tarragon), and a sprig of chervil (or a pinch of dried chervil) in a pan with 4 to 5 tablespoons of wine vinegar and half as much water. Bring to a boil and boil for several minutes. Put through a strainer. Put 4 egg yolks in the upper part of a double boiler and place over hot, but not boiling, water. Gradually add the strained liquid, beating constantly with a wire whisk. When the sauce has thickened, add 4 tablespoons of softened butter, one at a time, and blend thoroughly. Season with salt to taste and a dash of cayenne.

To serve: This is a classic accompaniment with broiled meats.

Makes about ⅔ cup sauce.

Variation

Chopped parsley and a bit of tarragon make an interesting addition to this sauce.

Blender Béarnaise Sauce

In a skillet combine 2 tablespoons of white wine, 1 tablespoon of tarragon vinegar, 2 tablespoons of chopped fresh tarragon or 1 teaspoon of dried tarragon, 2 teaspoons of chopped shallots or onion, and ¼ teaspoon of freshly ground pepper. Bring liquid to a boil and cook rapidly until almost all of it evaporates. Strain and pour remaining mixture into the Blender Hollandaise Sauce (page 208), cover, and blend on high speed for 4 seconds.

Makes about ¾ cup sauce.

Seafood Cocktail Sauce

1 tablespoon prepared horseradish	¼ teaspoon Tabasco sauce
1 tablespoon Worcestershire sauce	1 tablespoon lemon juice
3 tablespoons catsup	¼ teaspoon salt

Mix ingredients thoroughly and chill well before serving.

Serves 2.

MARINADES

Tenderizing Marinade

This is one of my favorites. Soak tough pieces of meat in this for 6 to 24 hours before barbecuing and see if you don't have delicious results. Use for basting as well.

½ cup olive oil
  or vegetable oil
½ cup soy sauce
½ cup bourbon
2 small onions,
  thinly sliced
2 cloves garlic, chopped

3 tablespoons chopped
  gingerroot or
  preserved ginger
1 teaspoon freshly
  ground pepper
1 teaspoon dry mustard
Dash of wine vinegar

Combine all ingredients and blend well.

Makes about 1½ cups marinade.

Shish Kebab Marinade I

1 cup red wine
½ cup soy sauce
1 cup orange juice
  or pineapple juice
1 teaspoon thyme
1 teaspoon rosemary
  seasoning powder

¼ cup Worcestershire
  sauce
1 cup finely chopped
  onion
1 teaspoon freshly
  ground pepper

Combine all ingredients and blend well.

Makes about 3 cups marinade.

Shish Kebab Marinade II

3 cloves garlic, crushed
1 tablespoon coarse salt
1 cup sweet sherry
1 cup orange juice
2 tablespoons vinegar
1 tablespoon basil

1 teaspoon rosemary seasoning powder
¼ cup chopped parsley
½ cup Worcestershire sauce
¼ cup brown sugar or honey

Rub the crushed garlic in the coarse salt. Combine all ingredients and blend well.

Makes about 3 cups marinade.

Shish Kebab Marinade III

1 cup soy sauce
1 cup pineapple juice
1 cup pineapple cubes
1 cup port or sherry
6 cloves garlic, crushed

1 tablespoon tarragon or tarragon seasoning powder
1 tablespoon freshly ground pepper

Combine all ingredients and blend well.

Makes about 4 cups marinade.

Javanese Marinade

1 cup soy sauce
1 cup sesame oil or peanut oil
1 cup chopped onion or shallots
3 tablespoons grated gingerroot or candied ginger

Chinese parsley or coriander seeds
Curry powder to taste
Pinch of cumin

Combine all ingredients and blend well.

Makes about 3 cups marinade.

Variation

Use half curry powder and half chili powder. Or add 1 cup brown sugar and 1 cup white wine to the marinade. This gives it an unusual flavor.

Hibachi Marinade

½ cup soy sauce
2 cloves garlic, chopped
2 tablespoons grated
  gingerroot or
  candied ginger

¼ cup brown sugar
½ cup sherry

Combine all ingredients and blend well.

Makes about 1¼ cups marinade.

Variation

Add curry powder to taste, monosodium glutamate, and a little chopped green onion or Chinese parsley (sometimes known as cilantro or fresh coriander; shop for it in Chinese, Mexican, or Puerto Rican neighborhoods).

Marinade for Game and Stew Meat

2 cups red wine
  Juice of 1 orange
  Juice of 2 lemons
1 large onion, sliced
8 peppercorns, crushed
  Sprig of thyme
1 teaspoon oregano
2 carrots, cut in quarters

  A few celery leaves
1 bay leaf
2 cloves garlic, chopped
¼ cup wine vinegar
½ cup olive oil
  or peanut oil
  Salt to taste

Combine all ingredients and blend well.

Makes about 4 cups marinade.

Variations

● If you like the Chinese style of flavoring, add 1 cup of soy sauce and 4 teaspoons of finely chopped ginger-root.
● If you like curry, add 2 tablespoons of curry powder.
● If you want an extra fine marinade, rub the meat with cognac, place in a large pan, and blaze it with ½ cup of warmed cognac; then pour your marinade over it.

DESSERT
& COFFEE

DESSERT

When you've had a hearty outdoors meal, you probably won't want a heavy dessert. Since most outdoor cooking takes place in the summer, you can take advantage of the abundance of good fresh fruit on the market. Some of these recipes may be prepared on the grill. In many, frozen fruits may be substituted for fresh.

Ice cream, of course, is a traditional dessert for outdoor meals, and toward the end of this chapter you'll find a list of both fresh and cooked fruits that make admirable toppings. They also may be used on Sour Cream Fruit Shortcakes (page 159), an admirable dessert.

Grilled Bananas

Select firm bananas, and slit each one through the skin and down one side. Do not peel. Put them on the grill and broil them in their skins until they are charred and soft to the touch. Using tongs, remove them to individual plates. Pass rum, sugar, and lemon and let each guest season his own.

Grilled Banana Flambé
Peel firm bananas and rub with sugar. Arrange on the grill and sprinkle with lemon juice. Broil until just delicately browned but not mushy. Transfer them to a flameproof platter, add another sprinkling of sugar, and pour ¼ cup of rum over them. Ignite the rum and carry blazing to the table.

Blueberries
Large ripe blueberries, chilled and served with maple syrup and sour cream, make a delicious and refreshing dessert.

Melons
Any kind of melon—well chilled—makes a perfect end to an outdoor meal. Melons require no advance preparation, they can be eaten out-of-hand, and they are all refreshing. If you like to dress them up a bit, pass port wine and let each guest add a dash to his own serving.

Peaches with Sour Cream
Peel and slice fresh peaches into a large bowl. Sprinkle with maple sugar or brown sugar or add maple syrup to taste. Just before serving, cover with dairy sour cream.

Peaches in Cognac
Peel and slice fresh peaches into a bowl and sprinkle with sugar. For 6 peaches add ⅓ cup of cognac and let stand for an hour before serving. For frozen peaches, allow about ¼ cup of cognac to a package.

Broiled Peaches

Either fresh or canned peaches may be broiled. If fresh, peel the peaches and split in half. Sprinkle them with brown sugar and broil, seed-side-down, for 3 or 4 minutes. Sprinkle the outside with brown sugar, turn, and continue broiling 3 to 4 minutes. Place a small dot of butter in the center of each peach half and add a little more brown sugar. Remove to a hot plate and blaze with cognac, if desired.

NOTE: Other fruits, such as pineapple, ripe pears, grapefruit, or bananas may be broiled over charcoal or you may combine various fruits on skewers for broiling.

Raspberries with Kirsch

Kirsch is a cherry brandy made in France, Germany, and in the state of Oregon. It is particularly good with all kinds of fruits. Merely a little sugar and a dash of Kirsch turns a simple fruit dessert into something special and glamorous. Try it on raspberries.

Raspberries and Pineapple

This is a wonderful combination. If you use frozen raspberries, let them thaw out over the pineapple—canned, fresh, or frozen. Add a dash of kirsch or cognac if you like.

Strawberries Jamaica

1	quart strawberries	1½	cups heavy cream
	Pineapple juice, slightly sweetened	2	tablespoons sugar Few drops of vanilla
¼	cup rum		

Hull the strawberries and cover with pineapple juice. Let them stand 1 hour and add the rum. Whip the cream, adding the sugar and vanilla.

To serve: Top the strawberries with the whipped cream.

Serves 4.

Strawberry Short Toast à la Helen Brown

This is an ideal outdoor dish. Toast slices of good homemade bread and butter them heavily. Cover with sweetened strawberries and serve with heavy cream, whipped or plain. I think you'll find this variation a welcome change from doughy shortcake.

Strawberries and Cognac

Stem fresh strawberries and cut them in halves. Sprinkle liberally with sugar and add ½ cup cognac for each quart of berries. Let them stand in a cool place for at least an hour before serving.

Strawberries Romanoff

This dessert has real elegance. If you don't keep a supply of liqueurs on hand, you can buy small individual bottles of these in most liquor stores.

1 quart strawberries	1½ cups heavy cream
½ cup sugar	Grand Mariner or
½ cup orange juice	Cointreau
½ cup port or sherry	

Hull the strawberries and arrange them in a serving bowl. Sprinkle them with the sugar, orange juice, and port or sherry. Let them stand for 1 hour. Whip the cream, flavored with a little Grand Marnier or Cointreau, and fold in.

To serve: As soon as the cream is mixed in, this dessert should be served.

Serves 4.

Watermelon Fruit Bowl

Choose a large ripe watermelon and cut a top slice off the long way, about one third of the way down. Remove the melon meat down to the last layer of pink, scooping it out so that the shell of the bottom section of the melon will form a big bowl. Cut the melon meat into cubes or into balls with a ball cutter. Add any other fruit you like to it—apricots, pineapple, strawberries, oranges, practically any fresh fruit will do—and mix it all together. Heap the fruit back into the shell until it is piled high. Add cognac or kirsch and chill melon well before serving.

Watermelon Supreme

This is a dish my mother used to serve frequently during the warm summer months and it was a great delight to all of us. Your guests will remember this dish for a long time.

Plug a fine ripe watermelon and pour in as much champagne as it will hold. Replace the plug and cover it with plastic tape. Cover the melon completely with ice. Or you can put it in your refrigerator if you have space for it. Let it chill for at least 12 hours—24 hours is even better.

To serve: Drain the champagne from the melon and cut it in wedges.

Ice Cream

America's favorite dessert, ice cream, is always good with an outdoor meal. It combines wonderfully with fresh fruits. Here are some suggestions for ice cream toppings.

Ice Cream Toppings

- Sliced sugared strawberries. Add whipped cream.
- Crushed sugared raspberries.
- Blueberries with maple sugar and a little sugar added.
- Sliced sugared peaches with brandy added.
- Pitted and sugared Bing cherries. Add brandy or kirsch.
- Sliced sugared nectarines.
- Sliced sugared apricots.
- Frozen pineapple or canned crushed pineapple with rum.
- Cooked fruit with a heavy syrup, fruit jam, or preserve.
- Cooked gooseberries with plenty of sugar.
- Sliced and sugared ripe figs.
- Fresh apricots cooked in a heavy syrup.
- Wild huckleberries cooked with sugar.

There are also the old standbys—chocolate or butterscotch syrup. Vary them by pouring some maple syrup over ice cream and sprinkling the top with pecans.

COFFEE

What wine is to the Frenchman, beer to the German, and tea to the Englishman, coffee is to the American. But despite the fact that the coffeepot is used more than any other utensil in the kitchen and on the campfire, its proper use is far too seldom understood.

The brew that you want—a fragrant, clear, flavorful coffee—is simple to achieve regularly if you take care with the procedure each time. In this way, you'll have uniform results—just as a good restaurant does.

First comes the coffeepot. There are dozens of different ones on the market, but they all belong to one of a few basic categories. There is the old-fashioned coffeepot, the percolator, and a variety of drip pots and vacuum devices. You'll find them in metal, glass, pottery, and porcelain. No matter which you use, the prime secret of making good coffee is to keep the pot clean. Unless your coffeepot is cleaned with soap and water and kept immaculate at all times, you cannot get a good brew.

The water is next in importance. Never take water for your coffee from the hot water tap, or you'll have flat-tasting brew. Use freshly drawn cold water. Especially in the morning, be sure you let the tap run a few minutes so you won't use water which has stood overnight in the pipes.

If you're camping or picnicking, you'll probably use the old-fashioned pot. Use a full coffee measure or two level tablespoons of coffee for each six-ounce cup of water. To ensure clear coffee by this method I always use a whole egg and shell for six cups. I mix the egg with the coffee and add the cold water. Let the coffee come to the boiling point but don't let it boil. Let it steep for a while. Add a few drops of cold water to settle the grounds. Serve it piping hot.

If you make boiled coffee at home over gas or electric grill, let it just come to the boil and then add a few drops of cold water. You need not use the egg for clarifying where the pot is subjected to less movement during the whole process.

For drip coffee, have a pot which is just large enough for the amount of coffee you want to make. I keep two or three sizes on hand—because you can't make two good cups of coffee in a six-cup pot. Measure the full coffee measure of drip-grind coffee for each 6 ounces of water. Bring the water to a rolling boil and pour over the coffee. When the coffee is dripped through, stir the coffee with a spoon to ensure an even brew.

There are several different roasts of coffee—the standard American roast, a French roast, which is roasted a bit longer, and the Italian black roast. Contrary to popular belief, there is no chicory in the black-roast coffees. Go to your small coffee dealer and he will show you the different roasts and grind them to your taste. I sometimes mix half French roast and half regular roast for a breakfast coffee, and use the black Italian roast for after-dinner coffee.

Fit your grind to your pot, and if you use different

kinds of pots, buy different grinds for them. Freshly ground coffee makes the best brew, and there are excellent electric grinders on the market which make short work of turning out the proper amount and grind of coffee for your needs.

I find that ground coffee keeps its freshness and flavor best if it's stored in the refrigerator.

All of these points are more important than the type of coffeepot you use. For indoor use, I favor the all-glass drip pot, with paper filters. Any sort of drip pot makes good coffee when kept clean and used at close to its top capacity. If you are careful about timing, a percolator does a good job, too.

Iced Coffee and Tea

These summer beverages are best when made from the freshly brewed product, poured hot over a glass full of ice cubes. Make coffee ⅓ stronger than usual; tea, twice as strong. Float heavy cream on top of your iced coffee if you like a rich drink. Add a sprig of fresh mint to each glass of iced tea—and try a slice of lime as a change from lemon.

SUMMER
BEVERAGES

In this chapter we take it for granted that you don't need to be told to have plenty of iced Cokes or Pepsis or a large pitcher of fresh-made lemonade on hand for the young fry at your outdoor party, as well as plenty of cold, cold beer and ale for the grownups to quaff with their food. We assume, too, that if you're serving non-drinkers along with those who like a cocktail or two, you'll provide the former with a tasty fruit- or vegetable-juice substitute. That old standby, tomato juice, can be pepped up considerably by adding a little lemon juice, ½ teaspoon of Worcestershire, and salt and pepper to each serving. Tomato juice is also good mixed with half-and-half with either sauerkraut juice or clam juice. And as a prelude to an outdoor seafood meal, there's nothing better than a small cup of ice-cold or piping-hot clam juice.

Now for the heartier drinks—the cocktails that sharpen appetites and the long thirst-quenchers for lazy summer days.

Bloody Mary

Vodka: 2 ounces
Tomato juice: 3 ounces
Lemon: juice of 1
Worcestershire sauce: 1 teaspoon
Tabasco: 1 dash
Salt and pepper: 1 pinch each

Like most drinks that have caught on, a Bloody Mary is drunk just about any time, but an afficionado will tell you there is no better time for one than after too many Bloody Marys the night before. To make: Shake the ingredients together in a shaker with cracked ice. Strain into a large glass. Dust with paprika or celery salt.

Champagne Cup

Champagne: 1 bottle
Brandy: 1 wine glass
Curaçao: 1 wine glass
Sugar: 1 tablespoon
Club soda: 2 bottles

Pour pre-chilled ingredients into a good-sized pitcher with a half-dozen ice cubes. Stir and serve. For a *Champagne Cocktail,* muddle 1 lump of sugar and 2 dashes of Angostura bitters in a chilled champagne glass. Add champagne to fill, twist and drop in a lemon peel. An even simpler drink is the *French 75*. To make: Put cracked ice in a 12-ounce glass until it is ⅓ full. Add 1 teaspoon of sugar, 1 tablespoon of lemon juice, 1½ ounces of gin. Muddle and fill to the brim with champagne.

Daiquiri

Light rum: 2 ounces
Sugar: 1 teaspoon
Lime: juice of 1

This is the basic warm-weather rum drink. To make: Shake ingredients with cracked ice and strain into a chilled glass. A *Frozen Daiquiri* is also made with light rum. It is poured without straining into a chilled champagne glass, the edge of which has been rubbed with lime peel and dipped in granulated sugar. A *Bacardi Cocktail* is a Daiquiri made with a teaspoon of grenadine instead of sugar. Dark rum is usually used to make a *Rum and Coke*, also known as the *Cuba Libre*. To make: Pour 1½ ounces of dark rum and the juice and peel of ½ lime into a 10-ounce glass. Add ice cubes and cola. For a *Rum Collins*, substitute rum for the gin of a Tom Collins (page 228).

Fish House Punch

Granulated sugar: 1½ cups
Lemon juice: 1 quart
Jamaican rum: 2 bottles
Cognac: 4/5 of a quart
Peach or apricot liqueur: 1 cup
Tea: 1 quart
Water: 1 quart

These ingredients will serve fifty. Scale down in proportion for a smaller number. To make: Let the sugar and lemon juice stand together until the sugar is thoroughly dissolved. Add the other ingredients, and let the whole mixture blend in a large punch bowl for 2 hours. About ½ hour before serving add a huge chunk of ice to the bowl and stir well.

Hawaiian Cooler

Vodka: 2 ounces
Pineapple juice: 2 ounces
Lime: juice of ½

A staple in a good many summer drinks is some form
of fruit juice. In most of the alcohol-fruit juice drinks
the method of preparation is the same: shake well with
ice and strain into chilled glasses. Another drink in this
category is the *Honolulu Cooler*. It is made with 3
ounces of light rum, 2 ounces of pineapple juice, 1 teaspoon of lemon juice, 1 dash of orange bitters, and
club soda to fill the glass. Another vodka variation is
called the *Cape Cod Cooler*. It is made with 3 ounces
of vodka, 2 ounces of cranberry juice, 2 teaspoons
sugar, and water or club soda. You can experiment with
endless variations of gin, or vodka, and the fruit juice
of your choice. If the result is not quite sweet enough,
in the next one try sugar or a teaspoon of one of the
cordials.

Mint Julep

Mint leaves: 6
Sugar: 1 teaspoon
Water: 1 dash
Bourbon: 4 ounces

Put 6 mint leaves in the bottom of a 12-ounce glass or
mug. Add sugar and water. Use a muddler or spoon
and crush the mint against the sides of the glass. Fill
glass to the top with very finely crushed ice, and pour
over this 3 ounces of the best bourbon. Stir and stir
untilt he glass begins to frost on the outside. Put it in
the refrigerator for a short time, being careful not to
rub the frost off with your hands. Just before serving,
fill again with crushed ice and add the other ounce

of bourbon. Decorate with sprigs of mint dipped in powdered sugar.

Moscow Mule

Vodka: 2 ounces
Ginger beer: 1 bottle
Lime: juice of ½

Put ice cubes in mug or highball glass. Pour in chilled ingredients. Garnish with cucumber peel. Gin may be substituted for vodka if you prefer.

Orange Blossom

Gin: 3 ounces
Orange juice: 3 ounces

If you haven't got fresh oranges, don't bother. The frozen variety might be all right for an appetizer at breakfast, but it is not good in drinks. To make: Shake with ice cubes and strain into a chilled glass. A derivative drink is the *Golden Screw*, vodka being substituted for gin. The *Screwdriver* is a Golden Screw that has been stirred instead of shaken. You can use rum instead of gin or vodka; you can stir or shake.

Planter's Punch

Jamaican rum: 3 ounces
Lime juice: 1 ounce
Sugar: 1 teaspoon
Angostura: 1 dash
Club soda or water: to fill

The Planter's Punch can be made and served in at least two different ways, depending on how much fuss and bother you think necessary. If you want a quick drink and easily made refills, pour the ingredients into a

12-ounce glass, add water, ice cubes, and serve. The other method is to shake well with cracked ice, pour without straining into a 10-ounce glass, fill with cold club soda, and top with a dash of nutmeg and an assortment of sliced fruit—to suit the eye and the palate. Serve this drink with straws.

Shandygaff

Beer: 6 ounces
Ginger ale: 6 ounces

Beer is the drink for the dog days. Whether from can, bottle, or keg, it should be poured cold so that it flows into a glass at a 45-degree angle. If and when you decide to try a mixed beer drink, try a Shandygaff. Pour chilled beer and ginger ale into a chilled 12-ounce glass. If you can get it, substitute ginger beer for ginger ale. Beer may also be drunk in a 50 per cent combination with ale, or ½ can of beer with 1½ ounces of chilled vodka, or in a drink called *Dog's Nose*, which is 1½ ounces of gin and a ½ can of beer.

Spritzer

Dry white wine: 1 bottle
Club soda: to taste

Fill a tall glass with ice cubes, pour in wine and soda until you have a combination that suits your taste. Red wine, sweet or dry, may also be used.

Stone Fence

Applejack: 3 ounces
Angostura: 1 dash
Cold cider: to fill

Pour ingredients into a highball glass with two ice cubes.

Another applejack drink for summer is the *Applejack Cooler*. It is made with 3 ounces of applejack, the juice of ½ lemon, a tablespoon of sugar. Shake vigorously with cracked ice and strain into a highball glass. Fill with chilled club soda. Lime may be substituted for the lemon.

Tom Collins

Gin: 3 ounces
Lime or lemon: juice of 1
Sugar: 1 teaspoon
Club soda: to taste

Gin is the main ingredient of the traditional Tom Collins, but a *Collins* may be made with vodka, rum, whisky, or any other liquor. To make: Put ingredients into a shaker with cracked ice and shake vigorously. Pour, ice and all, into a tall chilled glass. Add more ice, and club soda to fill. Decorate with cherry, slice of orange, lemon, or lime. Serve with straws. A variation of the Tom Collins is the *Gin Rickey*. It is made without sugar and is served in a medium-sized glass. A *Gin Sling* is a Tom Collins with 1 teaspoon of grenadine instead of sugar, and the ingredients are poured into a glass, then stirred slightly. A *Singapore Sling* is a Gin Sling with 1 ounce of cherry cordial for grenadine.

Vermouth Cassis

Dry vermouth: 3 ounces
Creme de Cassis: 1 ounce
Club soda: to taste

Dry vermouth—an important, if underrated, ingredient of Martinis—may be drunk by itself over ice cubes with a twist of lemon peel, or in a Cassis. To make the latter, pour ingredients into a highball glass filled with ice cubes. Other white wines may be substituted for vermouth.

Whiskey Sour

Whiskey: 2 ounces
Lemon: juice of 1
Sugar: ¼ to 1 teaspoon
Angostura: 1 dash
Club soda: to fill
Slice of orange or lemon
Cherry

A sour to be good does not have to be made according to a strict formula. It is not a finicky drink. It may be made with any of the whiskeys—some even say with rum, gin, or vodka. It may or may not have a slice of orange, a cherry, a dash of bitters. However, it must be shaken vigorously. To make: Put first four ingredients in a shaker with cracked ice, shake and shake some more, strain into a chilled whiskey sour glass, add club soda, and decorate.

INDEX

234

M